T0065104

THE WINE LOVER'S APPRENTICE

WORDS OF WISDOM FOR WOULD-BE OENOPHILES

KATHLEEN BERSHAD

Skyhorse Publishing

Skyhorse books may be purchased in bulk at special discounts for sales promotion, corporate gifts, fund-raising, or educational purposes. Special editions can also be created to specifications. For details, contact the Special Sales Department, Skyhorse Publishing, 307 West 36th Street, 11th Floor, New York, NY 10018 or info@skyhorsepublishing.com.

Skyhorse® and Skyhorse Publishing are registered trademarks of Skyhorse Publishing, Inc.®, a Delaware corporation.

Visit our website at www.skyhorsepublishing.com.

10 9 8 7 6 5 4 3 2 1

Library of Congress Cataloging-in-Publication Data is available on file.

Cover design by Jenny Zemanek
Cover illustration by iStockphoto

Hardcover ISBN: 978-1-5107-3161-5
Ebook ISBN: 978-1-5107-3165-3

Printed in China

For my grandpa Max

Contents

I

Get Your Wine Geek On

A Note from the Author

Here's a confession that won't be shocking: I'm a wine geek.

More specifically, I was a food writer who got into wine, studied at the American Sommelier Association, and worked at two wine stores, as well as a variety of importers and distributors, before striking out on my own. Today, I am a consultant, helping people buy, sell, and organize wine, as well as teaching and writing about it. And, when it comes to wine, I've heard it all:

"I love this kind of wine." [offers sip] "How do I describe it?"

"Can you tell me the basic wine grapes and what they taste like?"

"What makes a white wine *white* and a red wine *red*?"

Okay, the guy who asked this last question was trying to be a smart-ass, but he brought up a good point that has a legitimate explanation. (Flip to Chapter one, pg. 7, for details!) All the people who have ever asked me questions about wine have had one thing in common: they were interested in learning more but weren't sure where to start. So many wine books include long-winded explanations of winemaking or nitty-gritty details about obscure regions that can make an expert's head spin—and a novice want to run fast and far.

This book strikes out in a different direction by offering simple explanations and easy-to-understand information for fledgling wine geeks. I realize that many oenophiles (wine experts) will be appalled that this book takes a complex topic like wine and distills it to its essence. But the sheer volume of information out there is, in fact, the reason why this small guide to the big world of wine is needed.

The ways in which you'll be able to use the information in this book are myriad. Feel free to dip into its pages for basic facts about major wine region such as Bordeaux, Napa, or Chianti. If you're looking for a crash course on the wine grapes you're most likely to encounter, check out Chapter three (pg. 15). If you're headed to an important business dinner, review the pages on ordering wine in restaurants so you can order with confidence and perhaps even a hint of verve. Or, one day, you might just decide to sit down and read it from cover to cover. That's okay, too. This book goes really well with your favorite wine.

Chemistry, Cost, and Color

In high school, I remember taking aptitude tests designed to match students' skills with possible careers. The results, of course, offered a series of common, respectable jobs: doctor, lawyer, journalist, engineer, teacher. None of these tests ever mentioned the less traditional (not to mention fun!) ways in which to apply those skills, such as becoming a toy designer, movie critic, or, say, winemaker. Which is a shame, because, had I known about that last option, I might have paid a *lot* more attention in chemistry class. For, you see, winemaking is simple chemistry:

$$C_6H_{12}O_6 + \text{Zymase} \rightarrow 2\,(CH_3CH_2OH) + 2\,(CO_2)$$

Yeah, that probably makes as much sense to you as it did to me in the tenth grade. Translated to English, it means that sugar plus yeast equals alcohol plus carbon dioxide. You read that right. Wine is the result of yeast gobbling up sugar and producing alcohol with a side of carbon dioxide. For this reaction to happen, wine grapes have to sit on the vine long enough to develop a certain sugar level (Brix in industry parlance) that will produce enough alcohol during fermentation to turn grape juice into wine.

If making wine only requires "stomping and mixing a bunch of grapes," according to a customer at the wine store where I once worked, then why does one bottle of wine cost seven dollars while another costs seventy dollars? (To set the scene: the store was located in New York City's Hell's Kitchen; the woman clutched a bottle in each hand, waving them over her head; and, while she didn't actually curse at me, she wasn't Little Miss Sunshine, either.)

Like anything, the cost is a reflection of attention to detail. The seven-dollar bottle was probably made with fruit that was machine harvested from high-yielding vines (i.e., ones with lots of grapes on them),

A Few Words about Brix

Brix is a way of measuring sugar levels in a grape, which is an indication of the wine's potential alcohol level. The term is named after Adolf Ferdinand Wenceslaus Brix, a 17th-century German mathematician and engineer who was the first to measure the density of plant juices. Sadly, his biographies do not indicate his favorite wine, or even if he drank at all.

or perhaps gathered by pickers who made one or two passes through the vineyard. Once picked, it's possible that leaves, stems, and other debris were sorted from the fruit. But sorting may not have happened at all; in that case, the whole harvest shebang—twigs, leaves, and anything else caught up in there—may have been dumped into huge vats for fermentation. (Don't worry: The wine was filtered in the process to remove all that schmutz.)

Any oak treatment the wine received (which influences its color, tannins, flavor, and/or texture) might have been done by pouring a bag of oak chips into the grape juice, versus storing the wine in expensive barrels to age before bottling. The fruit used to make the seventy-dollar bottle, however, may well have been handpicked from low-yielding vines, which are considered better because they can concentrate more energy on fewer grapes, thus improving their flavor and quality. Also, it takes more than a few guys making one pass through the vines to pick all the fruit. A vineyard might have one hundred or more pickers who spend three or even four weeks among the rows to get each grape at its optimal ripeness.

Then, the grapes are sorted by hand (or a sophisticated machine) to remove the stems, leaves, and debris before being put into tanks. The juice may also be fermented in smaller batches, perhaps with carefully selected, more expensive yeasts. At this level, any oak aging would probably be done in barrels. A new barrel that holds enough wine to make twenty-five cases can set a winemaker back at least seven hundred dollars—and often much more.

These facts alone explain the reason for the cost differential between cheap and expensive bottles, yet anyone paying attention will notice that differently priced wines taste different, too. Less expensive wine might taste good but will be fairly basic in its flavors and feel. You might pick up a fruit flavor or two on the nose, and these will probably echo on your tongue when you take a sip—maybe blackberry for a red or apple for a white. But it will be hard to find other flavors, and the first and final sips from the glass will taste more or less the same. A pricier wine will also taste good but offer more distinctive flavors and aromas. The red might smell of cherry and spice, with flavors evoking cola, mushrooms, and licorice. A white wine could evolve from apples and pears to caramel, lemon, and almond. The flavor will change in the glass, surprising you along the way.

Which brings us nicely to wine flavors, another subject I get asked about a lot. A wine doesn't taste like apple because someone put apple juice in it. Instead, flavors come about because of the complex interplay between yeast, alcohol, oxygen, and sugar when fermenting the juice. These interactions produce esters—chemistryspeak for flavor compounds. It just happens that these esters are the same as in other foods we eat. For example, Beaujolais Nouveau tastes like banana because the winemaking process results in the same esters that give an actual banana its flavor.

That's all well and good, you say, but what about other wine words that get bandied about—acidity, minerality, or fullness? Where do those qualities come from? Again, there is no one reason, but rather a combination of factors that comprise the taste of a wine, including grape (each has its own characteristics), soil type, climate, elevation, winemaking technique, barrel selection, barrel toastiness, and more.

So, if all of those things influence taste, what gives a wine its color? The simple answer: the skins. Obviously, white grapes are used for white wine and red grapes for red (the answer my smart-ass friend in the introduction was expecting). But it's more complicated than that. Color develops over time when the juice soaks with the skins during the aging process. To wit: Orange wine is a trend that comes around every few years. It is made by leaving juice from white grapes in contact with the skins, thus creating that particular color. Red wine works the same way: the longer you leave the juice with the skins, the more color is absorbed into the liquid. A short amount of skin contact—from a few hours to, say, two days—will result in a pink or slightly red wine. A week of skin contact will result in a notably richer, deeper color. You can even make a white wine from red grapes by eliminating skin contact altogether. That's how the folks in Champagne make blanc de noirs wine—a white bubbly from red pinot noir grapes. But the color is also influenced by the thickness of a grape's skin. A thin-skinned grape like pinot noir produces wine that is noticeably light. Hold a glass up and you can read through it. In contrast, a thicker-skinned grape like cabernet or shiraz makes dark wines that can be completely opaque.

Fermenting Grapes.

Before we move on, I'd like to throw in a few words about red wine headaches, a question that comes up at pretty much every tasting I do. Sulfites usually get the blame, though most experts dispute this notion. Sulfites naturally occur in wine, as well as in tea, dried fruit, and a lot of processed foods. So, if you consume any of those products without problems, sulfites are not the cause of that migraine. Plus, white wines generally have more sulfites than red. The known cause of these headaches—which are common enough to have been dubbed red wine headache (RWH)—remains uncertain. Some think it's the tannins in red wine. It could also be histamine or tyramine (found in fermented foods), both of which have a nasty way of constricting and dilating blood vessels. There are lots of theories floating around, so if red wine really gives you headaches, try taking either an antihistamine or a pain reliever before imbibing. (Of course, check with your doctor first.) If that doesn't work, you probably need to avoid red wine altogether.

What You're Tasting When You Taste Wine

Some wine connoisseurs (not me) can taste or sniff a wine and detect, say, the scent of a Meyer lemon that was picked at 7:43 a.m. on a dewy morning by a left-hander.

That's nice, but who cares?

Having said that, it is good to know a little bit about what's in the glass beyond, say, "It's a red wine!" or "Oooh! Champagne!" A wine's character is created by a complex interplay between natural and human influences. There are ways to gather intel on these variations and figure out what's going on in the glass. And, bonus! With this information, you can reverse-engineer things, taking a few facts from a wine label or a menu to make an educated guess about what the wine will probably taste like. Here are some clues to look for:

New or Old? (And I Don't Mean Vintage!)

Old World and New World are two of the most common descriptors for wines. But a lot of folks don't know what those terms really mean. At its most basic, this distinction refers to the origin of the wine. As you might expect, Old World wines come from traditional winegrowing areas, such as France, Germany, Italy, and Spain. (In other words, Europe!) New World wines are from newer regions, where winemaking goes back a few hundred years or less. The best known of these are California and Australia, though the category also includes Chile, Argentina, Washington, Oregon, and New Zealand. (Basically, everywhere else!)

Each region produces wines with different characteristics. Overall, New World wines are higher in alcohol and have fruitier flavors than their Old World counterparts, which are typically more austere and reserved. But beware: thanks to winemaker manipulation (or factors like a warm vintage in a cool climate), an Old World wine can be crafted in a New World style, and vice versa.

Workers at the Hastings Ranch Vineyards in Pasadena, California, in the late 19th century. Courtesy of the Archives, Pasadena Museum of History.

Is It Hot in Here?

Climate plays an important role in viticulture, with a combination of sun, fog, temperature, and weather strongly influencing the outcome of a harvest. Warm climates have consistent temperatures throughout the growing season, allowing grapes to ripen fully but with less acidity. Cooler regions may be hot during the summer but then become cool around harvest time in the fall, preserving acidity but slowing the ripening process.

Perhaps coincidentally, New and Old World wines divide neatly across climate. Old World areas are cooler overall. If you remember your facts about Brix, you know that wine from these regions has less sugar and alcohol. As a result, these wines tend to be more mineral-based (think stones) in flavor and have a lean quality to them. In contrast, New World regions are generally warm, so wines are fuller and richer on the palate, with lots of fruit flavors.

Of course, it's not quite as simple as that. (You knew this was coming!) Factors such as elevation or proximity to water can impact a region, creating microclimates that might be significantly warmer or cooler than the surrounding areas. For example, the Chiles Valley District in Napa sees relatively hot days, with temperatures hovering around eighty-five degrees Fahrenheit. However, the vines are planted at eight hundred to 1,300 feet, which causes nighttime temperatures to plummet to slightly above freezing. As a result, grapes develop notable acidity compared to fruit from nearby Oakville, which is planted between seventy-five and five hundred feet in elevation.

Though we've been talking about the impact of climate on flavors, air temperature can also affect how a wine smells. Warm climate wines have a softer and riper, but less defined, perfume than those from cool regions, which offer crisper, more intense aromas.

To Oak or Not to Oak?

This topic causes one of the great divides in the wine world! A lot of people hate overly oaked wines, and the blame for this can be traced to the overzealous use of oak by California winemakers back in the 1970s. Though sometimes maligned, oak actually plays an important role in winemaking, as it impacts a wine's color, flavor, and tannin level. And for some grapes, interaction with oak is essential to creating a wine with structure, flavor, and ageability.

The various types of oak used to age wine offer their own unique characteristics. French oak, for example, offers silky tannins and savory notes with hints of clove and black pepper; American oak adds dill, coconut, and clove to the wine; whereas Slovenian oak imparts walnut tones. In addition, wines aged in French oak are usually more tannic than those aged in other types of oak, while American oak helps bring more intense flavor to a wine.

"Toast" is another way oak contributes flavor to the wine. When the barrel is being made, the producer can use open flame or an oven to char the inside of the wood. A wine that sees time in a lightly toasted barrel will have a dry, piquant spiciness, while one aged in a medium-toasted barrel offers sweeter notes of coconut and vanilla. A heavily toasted barrel can include hints of roasted coffee, smoked bacon, cloves, and even resin or tar. And, while many winemakers use new oak for their

A cement vat at Riecine, a stylish, modern winery in Chianti.

aging barrels, some choose to use barrels that are one, two, or more years old, as they offer a more restrained oak influence on the final product.

Although most people think "barrels" when they hear "oak," these containers aren't the only choice available to winemakers. There are numerous other, less pricey ways to oak a wine, including chips, dust, blocks, and staves—essentially large sticks of wood—that can be had for a fraction of the cost of barrels.

Okay, that is a *lot* of information about oaked wines. How about the unoaked variety?

So glad you asked.

If winemakers eschew oak, they are likely to use stainless steel containers or, less typically, cement vats for fermenting and aging wine. Both of these containers are considered neutral, allowing the wine to develop without any outside influences. This technique lets the wine's fruit flavors shine through. Such wines also offer a certain freshness and light feel on the palate, unencumbered by the effects of oak. Cheeky winemakers often refer to their unoaked chardonnay as "naked." Tee-hee!

Legs: Do You Know How to Use Them?

Swirl your glass (preferably with wine in it!), then look at the far side. Do you see "legs" of wine dripping down? Their presence tells you simply that the wine has relatively high alcohol content (and is thus from a warm climate or possibly vintage) or high sugar levels (e.g., a dessert wine). Contrary to once-conventional wisdom, legs aren't a quality indicator.

True Colors

Tilting the wine glass to examine color, though a cliché of the snooty wine drinker, can actually tell you quite a bit about the wine. For starters, color offers a clue to the wine's age. Look at the meniscus—the outer rim of the liquid at the far side of the glass. A young white wine will be a pale yellow or show a touch of green in its youth. This outer color darkens to brown as the wine ages. A similar process occurs with red wines, changing from bright purple or ruby to brick red and eventually brown over time.

Color can also tell you if you're going to get a light-bodied wine or a fuller, richer one. The former has light colors—think sauvignon blanc or pinot noir —while a darker wine—chardonnay or syrah—is more voluptuous. Finally, color also offers clues as to the region where the wine is from. Riper, warm-climate grapes tend to produce wines of deeper color, while the opposite holds true for cool-climate varietals.

Digging Up Dirt

The French notion of terroir (terr-wahr) suggests that the soil in which a vine grows gives the wine its character. In other words, you should be able to tell from one sip where a wine was made. (Yeah, that's not me, either.) Terroir is somewhat controversial; it's not hard to find an expert to call BS on it as more of a chic-sounding marketing tool than actual, provable fact. However, some correlations between soils and wines have been demonstrated.

For example, wine from clay soil can feel heavier in the mouth, with a fatty richness that gives it a savory touch, while slate soil imparts a zingy acidity to wine that is bracing and refreshing. Limestone soil offers minerality and a touch of acidity to wine. Gravelly soil also offers mineral tones, but wine from this soil is generally less acidic.

In a nutshell, then, matching a grape to the proper soil for that varietal results in the best possible growing environment.

A great example of this process is the syrah grape in France's Rhône Valley. How does the thick-skinned grape thrive in the area's windy, cool climate? Galets, thank you very much. These are large stones found in the soil that absorb the sun's heat during the day and reflect it back on the vines at night, giving them the extra boost of heat to grow

Galets at a vineyard in Châteauneuf-du-Pape.

robustly. Now, imagine the delicate, thin-skinned pinot noir planted in that environment. The grapes would love the cool weather but over-ripen with the reflected heat—a poor match of grape to soil.

This discussion suggests that different types of soil are fairly monolithic, but that's not the case. Most soil is a mix of, for example, clay and limestone, or gravel and schist. The exact composition can vary

THE WINE LOVER'S APPRENTICE

considerably within a vineyard, and even over a distance of a few hundred feet.

That Delicious Buttery Flavor

Though "buttery" is often paired with "oaky" in relation to California chardonnay, it is a quality all its own. The buttery flavor in some wines is a result of winemaker intervention and occurs during a fermentation process that is induced to convert stronger malic acid (think tart apple flavor) into smoother lactic acid (think milk). This process is, logically, referred to as malolactic fermentation, or "malo" in winespeak.

Wines can undergo full or partial malolactic fermentation, depending on the intent of the winemaker. The process is essential for certain types of wines, such as cool-climate reds with excessive acidity. It is also used for many white and some sparkling wines. In warmer climates or hotter years, the process will sometimes be suppressed to maintain a wine's acidity.

Get to Know Your Grapes

There are 1,271 primary wine grape varietals in the world, according to *Which Winegrape Varieties are Grown Where? A Global Empirical Picture* by Kym Anderson. A professor of economics at the Wine Economics Research Centre at the University of Adelaide, Australia, Anderson helped establish the academic program in 2010.

After that mouthful, you will be glad to know I am not going to offer tidbits on every single one. Instead, this chapter highlights what I consider the top nine red and white wine grapes based on what you're likely to see at a store or on a restaurant menu. Before we get started, it's important to reiterate that dozens of factors can impact a wine's flavors, which is why two chardonnays or malbecs can taste completely different. However, most grapes have certain qualities that show up in wines regardless of outside influences, and it is those characteristics that are described here, along with some of the regions that produce the classic versions of these wines.

Red Grapes

Cabernet franc is lighter in flavor than cabernet sauvignon, producing wines that are rich and intense with flavors of raspberry, blackcurrant, and graphite as well as the occasional vegetal note. This grape is most commonly found as part of a Bordeaux blend or on its own from France's Loire Valley.

Cabernet sauvignon is known for its notes of black currant and bell pepper. It makes a full and tannic wine that can also show flavors of mint, dark cherry, tobacco, or plum. While Bordeaux and Napa showcase this grape at its finest, cabernet is grown and vinified around the world.

Grenache is a soft, easygoing grape with notes of raspberry and strawberry, and a hint of sweet pepper. It is often blended; the best of these grapes are from France's Rhône Valley or used in Australia's GSM grapes—but can be found on its own, usually in Spanish wines. (GSM, by the way, is a blend of grenache, syrah, and mourvèdre grapes.)

Malbec grapes are bold, juicy, and tannic with notes of blackberry, tobacco, and violet. Once an important part of Bordeaux blends, the grape is nearly impossible to find there today. Winemakers in Argentina have laid claim to this varietal, and most of the world's malbec grows there.

Merlot is better known for its velvety texture than any particular flavor, but look for notes of red fruit, plum, cedar, and chocolate. As with cabernet, merlot is an essential grape for Bordeaux but is made into wine in virtually every region around the globe. Look in particular for bottles from Chile.

Pinot noir has light tannins and red fruit notes—think strawberry, raspberry, and cherry. But it can have meaty, earthy, or mushroom flavors, too. The best of its wines are from Oregon, New Zealand, and France's Burgundy region.

Shiraz or syrah (one grape, two spellings, both unrelated to petite syrah) is highly tannic and acidic with notes of blackberry, chocolate, and smoked meat. The two classic regions for wines made from this grape are Australia and France's Rhône Valley.

Tempranillo (temp-ra-knee-oh) shows notes of plum, strawberry, tobacco, leather, and herbs. This grape is primarily associated with Spain, and the best versions are from that country's Rioja (Ree-oh-ha) and Ribera del Duero regions.

Zinfandel produces a juicy, jammy wine with notes of raspberry, blackberry, and pepper. This is the quintessential California wine; earthy versions come from Italy, where the grape is known as primitivo. (Note that this is a hearty red wine, not the pink blush known as white zinfandel—a completely different animal!)

White Grapes

Chardonnay ranges from lean and crisp (think white fruits like apples and pears) to full and lush with more tropical fruit flavors (such as fig, banana, and mango). The best of its wines are arguably from Burgundy or California, but good versions are made in pretty much every wine-producing country in the world.

Chenin blanc is crafted in a variety of styles (dry, sparkling, sweet) thanks to its crisp acidity. The wines made from these grapes show notes of quince, apple, honey, and white flowers. The best of these are from South Africa and France's Loire Valley.

Muscat is known for its sweet, floral aroma and (forgive me, but it's true) grapey flavors. This grape is also known as moscato or moscatel. Look for ones from Italy and France.

Pinot blanc is full-bodied and acidic, showing flavors of apple and citrus, as well as floral notes. Still versions are found from Italy, France, and Oregon; California winemakers use the grape in sparkling wine.

Pinot gris is rich with pear, apple, and melon. When styled as pinot grigio, the wine is lean and crisp with very soft flavors. Its wine is produced globally, though Italy, Australia, Oregon, and California are perhaps the best sources for this wine.

Riesling (we're talking the dry or off-dry style here) shows floral-fruit notes and a slight whiff of petrol. Its bracing acidity gives it a crisp feel. The best of these are from Germany, France, and Washington State.

Sauvignon blanc is known for its fresh, grassy flavors. Seek out its wines from Bordeaux, Australia, California, New Zealand, or the Loire Valley.

Sémillon (say-mee-yon) makes both dry and sweet wines that have notes of apricot, peach, and nectarine. The grape is blended with sauvignon blanc to make white Bordeaux or is made on its own with great success in Australia, Chile, and Argentina.

Viognier (vee-own-yay) makes a round, luscious wine whose flavor is sometimes compared to chardonnay. It has notes of peach, pear, and violet. The Rhône Valley, Australia, and California all produce stellar versions of this wine.

Conquering the Restaurant Wine List

Remember the game "hot potato" that requires a small item to be quickly passed around, and whoever is holding it when the timer buzzes is "out"? The grown-up version requires a wine list and a group that's out to dinner. The list is handed to one diner and then quickly passed around until it lands in front of the person at the table who is deemed the wine connoisseur.

I am not making this up.

My friend Susan is constantly amazed that, even with her "slightly higher than Joe Schmo amount of wine knowledge," she is

This doesn't have to be you!

pegged as the expert who winds up selecting wine for the table. Other friends who have taken wine classes report a similar phenomenon. Heck, I've spent the last ten-plus years ordering wine for my husband despite his finicky taste and extensive wine knowledge because, in his words, "You're the trained sommelier."

Clearly, ordering wine at a restaurant ranks right up there with public speaking and first dates when it comes to stressful social situations. What if one person orders Dover sole while everyone else got a porterhouse steak? Can the wine satisfy the person who only drinks one brand of pinot noir that, of course, isn't on the menu? Is there a white wine on the menu to please both the sauvignon blanc-only and chardonnay-only drinkers in the group?

Fortunately, there are some easy ways to solve this particular social bugaboo.

Do Some Reconnaissance

The easiest way to get a handle on things is to look at the restaurant's wine list in advance. Many restaurants post them online, but I've been known to head to the establishment early (an hour or even a few days, depending on circumstances) to sit at the bar and peruse the list over a cocktail. This preview lets you review prices to find a good value (myriad websites and apps offer competitive pricing information) and research vintages if, say, that older Bordeaux is of interest. Doing this research gives you a general sense of what to order and the opportunity to meet the sommelier (somm-il-yay) in advance; you can let him or her know if the dinner is a special occasion (a proposal) or important event (a job interview).

Read the Headlines

Let's imagine that a sneak peek at the wine menu didn't happen. Instead, you are seated at the table looking at the list for the first time. Take a deep breath and take a broad survey of the menu to see how the list is organized. Typically, wines will be grouped by region or varietal, which allows you to narrow down the search to an area or grape that you like. A fan of shiraz? Head to the Australia or Rhône section. Prefer rich, full white wines? Look for chardonnay from California or white Burgundy from Corton-Charlemagne or Montrachet.

Go Broad or Go Home

Okay, you obviously can't ditch dinner for the comfort of your sofa, so if you're selecting for a large group with diverse tastes, think versatility. Several grapes produce wines that pair well with a wide array of foods, so you don't have to worry too much about the fish/meat dichotomy. These wines provide a middle ground, palate-wise. They aren't too big or too tannic or too fruity or too oaky or too anything that is potentially polarizing for your dinner companions.

The grapes to look for include: pinot noir, particularly from Burgundy, New Zealand, or Oregon. Pinot blanc/bianco from Oregon or Italy's Friuli or Alto Adige regions. (Note that this is a different wine from pinot grigio, which should be avoided at all costs because the good bottles are hard to pluck from the vast sea of mediocre ones.) Cabernet franc (red grape) or chenin blanc (white grape) from France's Loire Valley. For the former, look for one from Saumur-Champigny or Chinon. For chenin blanc, try one from Savennières, Anjou, or Vouvray. Grenache, which can sometimes be found bottled on its own or as a blend with shiraz, mourvèdre, and other grapes. Look for a bottle from Spain (where it's called garnacha), the Rhône, or Australia (on its own or as part of a GSM cuvée).

Merlot is maligned but a sure-fire crowd-pleaser. Look for a high-end one from California, or a Bordeaux from Pomerol or St.-Émilion. Chardonnay can be a polarizing grape, but ones from Burgundy generally lack the oaky, buttery qualities that bedevil some California chardonnays, and they are very lovely to enjoy with a meal.

Vintage, Schmintage

Seriously. Don't stress at all about vintage. For everyday drinking wines, factors like improved winemaking techniques have made vintage—the date on the bottle that indicates the year the grapes were harvested—more or less irrelevant.

Don't be mistaken: vintage matters, particularly for expensive wines or ones made from finicky grapes like pinot noir. But if you're ordering by the glass or an inexpensive bottle, giving the issue even a moment's thought just isn't worth your time.

If you are looking for a fine wine, however, keep in mind that the restaurant's wine staff does most of the work for you. It is part of their job to seek out good wines, even from bad vintages, thus minimizing diners' risk.

Further, a restaurant that doesn't have a wine director or strong wine list is likely to have a lot of wines that, because of the winemaking style at the estate, are probably going to taste the same or similar year after year.

Generalizations Are Good

A basic understanding of climate can also help you to identify wine styles and what you're going to get in a given bottle. Warmer climates tend to produce wines that are a bit fuller, more luscious, and fruitier—think California, Australia, Chile, Argentina, Spain, France's Languedoc-Roussillon region, and southern Italy. Wine from cooler climates, inversely, tends to be leaner and more austere. This applies to areas like Burgundy, Bordeaux, northern Italy, Oregon, Washington, and cooler California regions like the Russian River Valley.

Specifics Can Be Useful, Too

Keep in mind the rule of specificity, which goes: The more precise the location, the greater the potential for a better quality wine. This is a particularly useful tool for France's Burgundy wines. Here's how it works. A Burgundy that is labeled, say, "Les Perrières" means that the grapes come from that particular vineyard, as opposed to a wine simply designated "Bourgogne," which means the grapes come from a larger geographic area.

The Price Is Right

Money talk is awkward in any situation, but it can be especially mortifying when ordering wine for the table. After all, you may not want to announce that you can only spend, say, seventy-five dollars or so per bottle. Luckily, you don't have to! Just point to a bottle in your price range, and a good sommelier will pick up on it. Any recommendations she then makes should be within ten to fifteen dollars of that price.

The former is likely to be a better quality wine because all the fruit is taken from a certain, probably well-looked-after, vineyard. As an analogy, think of a New Yorker who lives in the upper reaches of Manhattan. He may boast about living in "Manhattan," while the Park Avenue denizen might flaunt that swanky address. And the person from across the river in New Jersey might confess to living "just outside" the city!

And, while I cite Burgundy, this guideline applies for pretty much any wine you see on a wine list. So, with these suggestions, and maybe a little help from the sommelier, you should be able to find the perfect bottle for your group —but it's not time to sit and relax just yet. After all, the sommelier is about to return with said wine.

Now you've come to the easiest part. First, check to make sure it's the wine you ordered, and that the vintage is correct. If not, simply say, "We ordered the 2014, not 2015." At this point, you may hear that the vintage changed but the list was not updated. Ask if the vintages are comparable and how the two wines differ. Also check to make sure that the price is the same. It often is, but doing so avoids any surprises when the bill comes.

Next, assuming you have the right bottle, touch it. Whether white or red, the bottle should feel slightly cool, indicating both proper storage and serving temperature. The right wine, the right temperature . . . so far so good. The sommelier opens the bottle, puts the cork in front of you (feel free to ignore it), and pours a little bit into your glass. Take a quick peek at the wine as you bring the glass up to your nose, making sure that it's clear, not cloudy.

Now comes the most important part: sniffing the wine. You're making sure it smells fresh and vibrant with bright fruit, floral, or other appropriate perfumes. If the wine smells flat or musty (some say dead flowers, wet newspaper, or moldy basement), then it is very likely bad. Though you can let the sommelier know it's okay to pour the wine at this point, it's usually good to take a sip anyway. This typically confirms the initial aromatic

Does it get any better than this?

23

impression, though on rare occasion, the wine might smell okay (or bor-derline) and still taste bad. You're looking for the same flaws as with smell—any old, musty, or flat qualities are not good. The wine should be vibrant and lively on the palate. However, if the wine is corked, or if you're not sure if it's bad, let the sommelier know that the wine seems off. She or he will probably sniff it as well, or may take the bottle away. Either way, a replacement bottle should be on its way to you. This is part of a sommelier's job, so there's no need to be bashful. (Seriously. I once sent three bottles back in a row, before the fourth was satisfactory. You'd think I might just have picked another wine, but, um, no.) Actually, I fibbed about this process being the easiest part. That honor really belongs to this last step: Sit back, drink, and enjoy.

Navigating the Wine Shop

Several years ago, I traveled with my aunt to take care of my sick mother. After a tough day, my aunt volunteered to pick up a bottle of wine so we could relax a bit. She returned with a slightly wild look in her eye, saying she wasn't sure what to get, so she went with the most expensive bottle in the store. Now, we were staying in small-town Minnesota (population a few hundred), so I wasn't expecting her to buy a three-hundred-dollar bottle. So maybe it cost thirty dollars?

Turns out, she bought a $10.99 bottle of Ménage à Trois, a California red blend that was just what we needed. Still, it was hard to believe an eleven-dollar bottle was the most expensive wine available! It made perfect sense the moment I walked into the store a couple of days later. Most of the alcohol selection was devoted to booze and beer, with

The Three-tier System

For the most part, wine gets to consumers in the US through what's called the three-tier system. The first tier is an importer, who brings a wine into the country and sells it to the second tier, a distributor. Then it is up to the distributor's sales staff to get these wines into the hands of retailers and restaurateurs—the third tier of the system—so they can get it to you.

one column of shelving devoted to wines—most of them contained in boxes or jugs.

That's one way to go when it comes to picking wine: buy the most expensive bottle. I've also had a surprisingly large number of people confess to regularly buying whichever wine has the prettiest or most eye-catching label. These are understandable strategies that I may or may not have engaged in a few times myself! After all, wine shops can be tricky to navigate. Maybe there's no signage to identify the California wines from the Italian ones, or everything is just muddled together. Plus, we humans are susceptible to the draw-your-eye-to-this-shelf tactics diabolically designed to steer us toward particular merchandise. We also have an unfortunate tendency to grab the first thing we see.

To wit: One store where I used to work had a huge display that faced customers right when they walked in. It was impossible to miss and was filled with magnum-sized bottles of an everyday pinot grigio that cost $7.99. One day, to mix things up, we decided to turn this display by ninety degrees, so that the bottles faced the cash register, not the door. And do you know what? Sales plummeted by half.

Needless to say, we turned the display back around.

The good news is, there are strategies you can use to overcome the temptation of displays. Find a wine shop you trust and cultivate a relationship with a particular staffer who gets to know your preferences. That way, you can breeze in and out, knowing that you will be satisfied with every purchase. For many, though, that's a pipe dream. The reality of shopping for wine isn't always so easy. For example, some states own the liquor stores, so selection is limited. Or, maybe you're in a small town without much wine culture, or at a store where the salesperson is less than helpful.

So the first rule is: Don't buy the first bottle you see!

Here's why: Distributors have what is called "allocated wines." These are highly limited bottles of highly desirable wines—maybe ten cases are available to distributors across the US, so the distributor conditions the purchase of these select wines on the retailer also buying a large quantity of a particular, lower-end wine.

For example, a retailer, in order to get six bottles of a high-end Burgundy, also has to purchase twenty-five cases of an $8.99 Australian shiraz. Guess what's going front and center with a big SALE sign?

Yep, the shiraz, bought only so the store could have the three-hundred-dollar wine to sell to its elite customers. For the record, that doesn't mean that the shiraz is a bad wine; it just may not be the best $8.99 wine for you.

Okay. Now you step in the door, bypass what's right in front, and are faced with rows and rows of bottles. What's next? Find the section of wines that matches your purpose. For example, if you want a nicer bottle to bring to a friend's party, go for something easy drinking but impressive, like a red Burgundy or Oregon pinot noir. Or, if you want something refreshing for a hot summer day, look for a crisp New Zealand sauvignon blanc or a light rosé from Provence.

Once you choose a region and grape, figuring out which bottle to pick is a process helped by economics. For example, Bordeaux and Napa are two areas known for their upscale, high-end wines. Do not, under any circumstances, reach for a ten-dollar bottle in these sections. They will be disappointing and leave you wondering what the big deal is about these wines. (Wine econ 101: the very best grapes go into the most expensive wines, and it trickles down from there.) From high-end areas like these, you can find something respectable starting at twenty dollars, but you really want to look at thirty dollars and higher for these sorts of wines.

Conversely, a bottle from a lesser-known region—let's say Portugal— is likely to offer a pretty decent value at ten or fifteen dollars in a way that an Oregon pinot won't.

For another perspective, consider the grape. Shiraz from Australia is going to cost more than, say, pinot noir from that country. So if you're debating between a fifteen-dollar Aussie shiraz and a fifteen-dollar Aussie pinot, go for the latter. Why? It's wine econ 101 at work again: shiraz is more popular, so the best grapes go into the premium wines. Pinot in Australia is less known, so relatively good-quality grapes are getting into that bottle, but because Aussie pinot doesn't have the same cachet, it can't command as high a price.

Another buying trick is to go for the exotic. This technique, again, is all about name recognition and branding: A twelve-dollar bonarda from Argentina will probably be way more interesting than a twelve-dollar California merlot, so when faced with a bin, table, or shelf of wines in the same price point, go for the one with the less familiar grape or region.

If you go to the same wine shop regularly, be sure to ask if they keep track of customer purchases, so next time you can find the same wine, or know what to avoid. This information allows the store staff to get to know your preferences as well and, over time, helps them make recommendations based on your palate. However, if the store doesn't track your purchases, pick one of the many wine apps out there and download it to your smartphone. It's an easy way to keep track of, review, and rank what you drink. Having this record will save you a headache in the long run. (Though, unfortunately, it is not the kind you get from drinking too much—that's totally on you!)

Serving, Sipping, and Storing

Client: "Should I get a single- or dual-zone wine refrigerator?"

Me: "Single is fine. Dual isn't usually worth the uptick."

Client, very skeptically: "Oookay."

I've had this conversation with disturbing frequency. It reflects the fact that, for most fledgling wine geeks, keeping and serving wine at home is a perilous proposition. It's not, but the notion seems to stick. Here's the reality: for the casual drinker, serving, sipping, and storing matters much less than you think. Let's start with serving. There's nothing to worry about when it comes to opening the bottle. Use whatever device floats your boat. My husband is enamored with the Rabbit wine bottle opener; I prefer using the traditional waiter's corkscrew, which is made with a double-jointed pull that makes it easier to get the cork out. A client of mine loves a simple electric corkscrew. The point is to get the bottle open any way you see fit. (Within reason!)

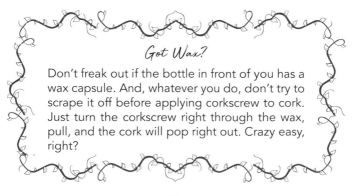

Got Wax?

Don't freak out if the bottle in front of you has a wax capsule. And, whatever you do, don't try to scrape it off before applying corkscrew to cork. Just turn the corkscrew right through the wax, pull, and the cork will pop right out. Crazy easy, right?

Next, you might want to think about decanting the wine—pouring it into a special pitcher designed to help bring out the wine's flavors and texture. Some people say it enhances the taste of any vino, from an eight-dollar bottle to an eight-hundred-dollar one. It can definitely make a difference, particularly if the wine has sediment, is a little older, or is very young and tannic. If you don't have a decanter (or are lazy like me and don't want to bother with washing it), then skip it, or get one of those little aerating gizmos and show it off!

To take the worst-case scenario, if you take a sip and the wine feels closed—in other words, not really flavorful—then swirl your glass around a few times so the wine can open up.

Which brings us to perhaps the most fraught of all questions about serving wine (and it seems like I've covered a lot of them thus far): what type of glassware should you use? Riedel makes a gorgeous line of stemware called the Sommelier Series. I have been lucky enough to drink wine from these glasses, and it tasted ethereal. The experience made me believe that the type of glass you use really does enhance the taste of wine. But I didn't love it enough to want to spend three figures per highly delicate glass. After all, if one broke, I would have a major meltdown over its replacement cost. Bottom line? You don't need to spend a lot of money for your wine glasses.

Next up, figure out what style of glass is important to you. After all, some companies make glasses by grape type: one for chardonnay, one for sauvignon blanc, one for merlot, one for pinot noir, and so on. Thankfully, being so specific is definitely not necessary. Don't get me wrong; if you have really high-end wines and an equally high budget (and lots of cabinet space!), then go for it. For most of us, though, just about any wine glass will be fine. That even goes for stemless glasses, whose practicality I understand completely. There's no fear of knocking one over, they are easy to hold, and they fit easily into the dishwasher. For me, though, I can't get past seeing all the fingerprints dirtying up the bowl! Speaking of bowls, does size matter? In fact, it does! You see, there are two key elements to wine glass design: the width and overall shape of the bowl. First, a larger bowl allows more oxygen to get into the wine, helping it to open up while in the glass, bringing out the aromas and flavors. This is particularly important for red wines, which is why red wine glasses are larger than white wine ones. Second, the nuances of the shape of the bowl (taller, wider) help direct the wine to the ideal areas of the tongue to maximize your ability to taste the flavors.

The more important question is, does maximizing the flavor of wine matter to you?

If yes, then invest in wine glasses to use for heavier and lighter reds (typically called Bordeaux and Burgundy glasses, respectively), as well as one everyday white wine glass. If no, then a single set of red and a single set of white glasses will get you through pretty much any occasion. And if the thought of even two sets is too much, keep it simple by buying all-purpose glasses that can accommodate both red and white wines. Problem solved!

You've poured, you've enjoyed, and you've got some wine left. Some wags would say just drink up and finish the bottle. But for fun, let's say that's not going to happen—the evening has ended and you've had your fill. Just put a cork (or vacuum stopper or whatever closure you have) in the bottle and put it in the refrigerator. Yes, even your reds. This slows oxidation and will give you a few extra days to finish drinking the wine before it goes bad.

An open bottle will keep in the fridge anywhere from two or three days to a week. This length of time is usually determined by the quality of a wine, so you can use price as a rough guideline. The more expensive the wine, the longer it is likely to last. (Tannins are a good clue, too. Red wines will keep longer than whites.) However, a regular refrigerator should never be used for long-term wine storage, say, more than a month. It doesn't provide the humidity needed to keep the cork moist, so it will shrink and thus cause the wine to oxidize—not the desired outcome. If you are the sort to buy and save wines, storing your unopened bottles in a wine refrigerator is best. (Absent a wine cellar, of course!) As mentioned above, dual-zone refrigerators don't make bottles last longer when storing. I had single-zone fridges for years, kept at about fifty to fifty-five degrees, and the wines were always fresh. If you don't have a temperature- and humidity-controlled place for long-term storage, at least keep your wine somewhere without wide temperature fluctuations and that is as dark and cool as possible. Also, keep bottles away from anything odorous, as, over time, these aromas can seep into the wine.

Storing wine brings us to another question I am often asked: how long can a wine age? Before answering, it's important to distinguish between a wine that can "age" and will change and evolve in the bottle over time, as opposed to one that will "keep," which means how long it will last before it turns bad.

A handful of wines—think high-end Barolo, Burgundy, and Bordeaux—can age and need that time in the cellar for the flavors to come together, sort of like a stew or pot of chili that needs to sit over-night for the flavors to really shine. However, most wines don't require aging and really should be enjoyed right away. But that doesn't mean they won't keep; as you probably know from experience, most of us have bottles that lie around for a while before we get around to drinking them.

The best guideline to go by is that white wines are generally good for two to three years after the vintage date, while red wines are good for three to five years. There are always exceptions. Many high-end Napa cabs, for example, can last for seven to ten years after the vintage date. However, precious few Champagnes will keep, so don't save the bubbly for a "special occasion." Instead, make tonight's dinner the special occasion and pop open that bottle you've been saving. In fact, take that advice for any wine you have shelved.

The Thirty-minute Rule

Most people serve wine at the wrong temperature. They keep red wines on the counter (to serve at "room temp") and put whites in the (real) fridge to cool down. But the result of those decisions is too warm reds and over-chilled whites that taste . . . well, pretty blah. So, unless you are drinking something straight from the wine refrigerator or cellar, please do this before popping the cork on a bottle: If the bottle is at room temperature, put it in the freezer for thirty minutes (no more!) before serving and if it's been in the fridge for a while, take it out about thirty minutes before you open it. Either way, the wine gets to a properly cool serving temperature, which allows its flavors, zippiness, and other such charming qualities to shine.

The Wine Regions

Whether you've read the whole book thus far, or picked this section to start your wine journey, let me welcome you to Part two! Getting to know the world's wine regions is the fun part. Although it can seem overwhelming, don't fear. This section focuses primarily on wine regions you know about or are most likely to run into at a restaurant or wine shop. After all, what's the point in discussing a place whose wine you'll taste only if you're driving among the Alps between France and Italy?

Even better, things are broken up so you can understand a wine region in just a few minutes. Here's how it works. Each chapter focuses on one country and starts with a quick intro to the area and its wines. The next sections tackle the major appellations within the country, dividing the details into three— sometimes four—categories: What You Need to Know describes the region's wine in one or two sentences; Grapes simply lists the major varietals; What to Look For details the wines produced in that region, as well as their primary characteristics, and suggests the best regions and the value buys; and More Details offers, in some cases, additional information that doesn't readily fit above but is useful for you to know.

That's it! Now, get reading . . .

Argentina

Argentina established its wine reputation on a red grape that is unfamiliar to most people: malbec (or, at least it was until the 1990s, when Argentine malbec reached peak popularity). But that's not the most unexpected aspect of this South American country's winemaking history. It's the fact that malbec is a French grape that was once essential in Bordeaux blends but today only plays a minor role in the country's wines. How did it take crossing an ocean and more than 150 years before the grape hit its stride?

As in much of the Americas, winegrowing was brought to Argentina by the Spanish colonizers. The first vines (they weren't malbec) were planted there in 1551, where they found a very hospitable home. The industry, such as it was, puttered along until the mid-1800s, when the country's expanded railway systems allowed for greater trade and commerce. Argentine winemakers could now easily get their wines to markets around the world. During this time, the country's first wine school was established, bringing modernized winemaking techniques and introducing French varietals (this is when malbec made its grand entrance) to the country's vineyards.

As fate would have it, the imported malbec vines thrived in this new environment. They produce a wine that showcases flavors and richness, quite the opposite of the often harsh and tannic French version. At its peak, there were 123,500 acres of the grape planted, though that number has been reduced to a little more than 95,000 acres as of 2014, according to winesofargentina.org. In contrast, there are fewer than 15,000 acres of malbec planted in all of France, and most of those vines are located in Cahors, a small town some one hundred miles east of Bordeaux.

Before moving on, it's important to mention Argentina's signature white grape, torrontés. This little guy grows primarily in Argentina, with just a handful of plantings found in Chile, Uruguay, and California. Funny enough, torrontés went unidentified for many years. Seriously, you ask?

Seriously.

Here's what happened. Two varietals brought over during colonial times cross-pollinated at some point, producing a new grape. The problem was, the new varietal apparently wasn't different enough from the surrounding vines for anyone to take much notice. (This happens more often than you'd think—see the section on Chile for a similar example!) However, by the mid-19th century, growers were onto this new varietal and dubbed it torrontés. (Note that Spain's torrontés is a different grape altogether.)

While malbec and torrontés are the national grapes of Argentina, growers are increasingly incorporating European varietals into their vineyards, including cabernet, syrah, chardonnay, and sauvignon blanc. Wine regulations are quite relaxed in Argentina, allowing winemakers significant latitude to experiment and follow their passions. In addition, wines in Argentina are assigned one of three quality designations. The first and simplest is IP (Indicación de Procedencia), which only requires that 80 percent of the grapes come from the region specified on the label. The second tier is IG (Indicación Geográfica). The grapes must be from—and the wines vinified and bottled in—their designated area. The highest quality wines are indicated by the DOC (Denominación de Origen Controlado) designation. Only two regions—Luján de Cuyo (lu-han de coo-sho) and San Rafael—have achieved that status. In truth, many of the country's IG wines are as good or better than DOCs.

Mendoza

What You Need to Know

Argentina's best-known region is a great source for everyday sippers.

Grapes

Malbec and torrontés rule in Mendoza, but many of the noble varietals—
most notably cabernet and chardonnay—are also made here, to excellent
effect. Though harder to find, bonarda is another native varietal worth a
try. It is fruity and lighter-bodied than malbec.

What to Look For

The best malbec in Argentina comes from the regions Luján de Cuyo
and the Uco Valley, both subappellations of Mendoza. However, the Uco
Valley is also gaining a reputation for stellar chardonnay. Maipú (not to
be confused with Chile's Maipo Valley) is a great source for cabernet
sauvignon, given its cooler climate.

More Details

These wines are known for being bold and richly flavored with lots of
juicy acidity. It's the latter quality that makes these wines very drinkable,
food-friendly, and quite popular with party guests!

A Is for Appellation: Wine Laws

Every government has laws and regulations that guide its country's wine industries. Some countries keep their requirements simple. They may legislate, for example, that a wine's grapes must be predominately from the region stated on the label, and, if a varietal is listed, it must comprise a substantial majority of the blend. The exact proportions vary but are usually somewhere around 75 percent. Other countries get into the nitty-gritty details of winemaking by ruling, for example, when grapes can be harvested, how many grape clusters to have per vine, and which winemaking techniques can or cannot be used.

Furthermore, certain designations that mean something in one country are totally meaningless in another. In Spain, for example, Reserva indicates that the wine received extra aging time. But in the US, the term Reserve has no legal definition but is used by winemakers to designate their highest-end wine. In addition, most countries also have what's called an appellation system. This hierarchy was originally created by the French to differentiate everyday table wines from more quality wines, and virtually all winemaking countries have adapted their own versions of these regulations.

Salta

What You Need to Know

This region's unique terroir creates torrontés wines that are truly breathtaking.

Grapes

Torrontés!

What to Look For

Salta is the overarching appellation and is quite an up-and-coming area for those in the know. Wines from the subappellations of Cafayate (caf-a-shada) and Molinos are also worth it, if you can find them.

More Details

Located in the northern part of the country, Salta has some of the world's most extreme vineyards. Vines are planted higher here than anywhere else in the world (none lower than 4,900 feet, a few climbing to more than 10,000 feet), but they also sit at twenty-four degrees latitude, a hot area that is at the upper boundary of winemaking in the southern hemisphere. These extremes average out, creating uniquely fresh and aromatic wines. Expect to find notes of peach and apricot with perhaps a hint of spice in wines from this region.

Patagonia

What You Need to Know

This region is known for its European-style chardonnays and pinot noirs.

Grapes

Chardonnay and pinot noir are the best tasting wines from this (literally) cool desert region.

What to Look For

The subregions of Río Negro and Neuquén (new-ken) produce particularly notable wines that are cool-climate varietals.

More Details

Patagonia, located at the other end of the country from Salta, has the southernmost vineyards in South America. They are notable for being

Understanding Elevation

Altitude is a point of pride among Argentine vintners, and there is an environment of one-up-manship to see who has the highest vineyards. European winemakers consider 1,600 feet the highest elevation suitable for grapes; in Argentina, vines are planted at twice that. What makes elevation so important? High-altitude grapes enjoy a cool climate that boosts acidity, while abundant sunshine elevates tannins. The resulting wines show unique concentration, structure, and roundness in flavor.

comparatively low in altitude, since the region lies at just 1,000 to 1,600 feet above sea level. As a result, these wines tend to be a touch earthier and less fruity than other New World wines. The best of them show an elegance and purity reminiscent of good French Burgundy.

Detail Map

Australia

By day, patrons of Sydney's Intercontinental Hotel might surf at Bondi Beach, stroll through the Royal Botanic Gardens, or catch a performance at the Sydney Opera House. By night, they sleep on another historical site. The hotel, you see, stands in the same spot where the country's first recorded vineyards were planted in 1788. From those few vines, a startlingly diverse industry took root. Since then, Australian wine has played a key role in many international wine trends. The 1950s and 1960s, for example, saw the production of "stickies," or sweet wines, that were particularly favored by the British. And the 2000s saw the enormous popularity of the "critter label"—a kangaroo, koala, or other adorable animal that adorned the packaging of simple, inexpensive wines. Don't think all Aussie wine is basic, though: the country also claims its share of high-end, cult, and collectible wines that stand shoulder-to-shoulder with the best from Bordeaux, Piedmont, or Napa. Penfolds Grange, for example, has spent decades as one of the world's most coveted and expensive wines.

In fact, one of the greatest qualities of Australia's winemakers is their unique style and freedom to indulge in it. Unlike many regions with very strict appellation requirements, Australia's regulations are pretty basic. The official food standards guide for Australia's wine industry—including dry, sparkling, and fortified wines—runs a whopping six pages long. (For perspective, the most recent US Federal Regulations on alcohol take up 886 pages!) Australian winemakers are free to plant vines wherever they see fit, not in a particular spot based on terroir, and can, should they choose, blend grapes from different regions into a cuvée that is often greater than the sum of its parts. The folks at d'Arenberg, an Aussie winery established in 1912, are some of the greatest practitioners of this art. A fine example is their "The Sticks and Stones" cuvée, a blend of tempranillo (a Spanish grape), grenache (French), and souzão and tinta cão (both Portuguese). The result is a melting pot of wines from mass-produced brands to top-notch premium labels—and a true success story.

Barossa Valley

What You Need to Know

Located near Adelaide in southeastern Australia, this area is the country's finest wine region and the home of big, bold shiraz.

Grapes

Shiraz is the major red grape, riesling the most notable white. Barossa Valley is also a great source for sémillon and chardonnay.

What to Look For

Barossa Valley is home to some of the best shiraz wines in the world. While they are worth every dollar spent, the region's winemakers also excel at crafting good wines at everyday prices. For white wine lovers, the subregion of Eden Valley is the go-to. Their riesling and chardonnay are particularly delicious, known for citrus and floral flavors.

More Details

Some of the oldest shiraz vines in the world are planted here. In fact, Barossa's Langmeil Winery is home to vines dating back to the 1840s. Wines made from older vines (usually considered fifty-plus years of age) are valued because they show particular depth and intensity. Regardless of vine age, Barossa shiraz is rich and heady with distinctive notes of chocolate and spice.

Yarra Valley

What You Need to Know

This region is Australia's answer to Burgundy, making it a great source for top-notch chardonnay and pinot noir. Lovely sparkling wine also is made here.

Grapes

It's no surprise that pinot noir and chardonnay are this region's primary grapes. Sauvignon blanc, cabernet sauvignon, and shiraz are also cultivated.

What to Look For

Yarra Valley is the go-to region for Aussie wines that are crisp, clean, and elegant.

More Details

Burgundy is famed for its refined wines made from chardonnay and pinot noir. Though warmer than the French region, the Yarra Valley offers a very hospitable environment for these cool-climate grapes. Yarra Valley wines are much lighter than their counterparts from other parts of Australia. The chardonnay can range in style from full, rich, and complex to lean, delicate, and minerally. Yet, they all show distinctive flavors of fig and white peach. Pinot noir lovers will find these wines have notes of strawberry and plum, with a depth of flavor that belies the wine's delicate nature.

Hunter Valley

What You Need to Know

Sémillon is this region's signature wine.

Grapes

Sémillon dominates this area, but chardonnay and verdelho (ver-day-ho) are also grown for white wine. It should be no surprise that shiraz is also quite popular.

What to Look For

For white wines, seek out the Hunter Valley designation. The subregion of Broke Fordwich is your go-to for cabernet sauvignon.

More Details

The best sémillon from this area is very age-worthy, keeping for ten years or more. The flavors change noticeably with time. Young sémillon is generally lean and angular with mineral and grassy notes, then becomes quite lush and rounded with notes of honey and biscuits. (Mmmmm!) Hunter Valley's finer shiraz, it should be noted, is also worth putting in your cellar. These medium-bodied wines show notes of game and leather in their youth, evolving into silky smoothness with earthy flavors reminiscent of their Rhône Valley counterparts.

McLaren Vale

What You Need to Know

Home mostly to boutique wineries, this small region has a big reputation.

Grapes

Shiraz is the most important red in the area, followed by cabernet sauvignon and grenache. Chardonnay and sauvignon blanc are the prominent white grapes.

What to Look For

McLaren Vale shiraz is notable for its deep purple color and flavors of berry and spice. For chardonnay, try to find some from the McLaren Flat subregion, which offer abundant acidity and richness.

More Details

Shiraz is the most important varietal by far, accounting for half of all grapes crushed each harvest. Winemakers typically blend fruit from the various subregions into complex, intensely flavorful wines hallmarked by berry, spice, and licorice notes. The best of these can age for twenty-plus years in the bottle. McLaren Vale is also a great source for Australia's GSM blends (made with grenache, syrah, and mourvèdre grapes). These wines are generally earthy and savory rather than fruity, with luscious chocolate and berry flavors.

Margaret River

What You Need to Know

Crafted in an old-world style, these wines are all about elegance and finesse.

Grapes

Bordeaux varietals dominate here—cabernet, merlot, and sémillon in particular. (Red grape, red grape, white grape, for those of you keeping track!)

What to Look For

Margaret River is a great appellation for affordable everyday wines. In addition to the grapes above, chenin blanc from this area is a well-kept secret. If you see a bottle, grab it!

More Details

This wine region is very young—major planting started in 1967—so the wines tend to be crafted in a modern and innovative style. There are roughly 215 growers and wine producers in the region, most of them smaller-scale. The climate is similar to Bordeaux, hence the large plantings of Bordeaux varietals, but don't overlook the chardonnay, shiraz, or sauvignon blanc from this area, either. Because the climate is more temperate than other Australian wine regions, these wines are less exuberantly fruity and more restrained in flavors and feel.

Clare Valley

What You Need to Know

This area is your source for crazy good riesling.

Grapes

In addition to riesling, sémillon is the other go-to white grape. Cabernet and shiraz are the most popular reds produced here.

What to Look For

Seriously, riesling.

More Details

Looking at the area's reds, think big and bold with lots of flavor. Crafted in a dry style, riesling from the Clare Valley is among the best in the world. Even better, these are hidden gems, as riesling from France, Germany, and California is better known and, typically, more expensive. (We're back to wine economics, remember?) If you think you hate riesling, think again. While some are sticky-sweet, the ones from Clare Valley don't even come close to being cloying. Instead, they are zippy, acidic, and minerally with notes of lime and orange blossom. What could be better?

California

It's probably no surprise that in low-key, let-it-all-hang-out California, the state's winemakers take a relaxed approach to wine—but they take their craft seriously, too. After all, this is where "Cali-Itali" (making fresh, California-style wine from Italian grapes) was invented and where the Rhône Rangers (irrepressible, break-the-rules winemakers who popularized classic Rhône varietals like syrah, grenache, and viognier) made their mark. California is also where lesser-known varietals have passionate champions and where (quite possibly) the word "naked" was first used to describe an unoaked wine. You can find anything there from high-end wines that cost three figures to box wine that'll set you back less than a ten-spot.

It all started when Spanish missionaries first planted vines here in the late 1700s. From that single vineyard sprang, over the next one hundred years, a thriving industry that was only stopped by something as extreme as Prohibition. Despite the ravages caused by the national ban on booze, the wine business came roaring back in the mid-20th century. Though this rebound started with bulk wine—think jugs labeled "Hearty Burgundy" and "Chablis" that bore no relation to the lithe and elegant French burgundies for which they were named—it now rests its laurels on top-notch wines—think Napa cabernet this time—that compete with the world's best.

But to distill California to one wine is an injustice.

The state is home to an amazing array of wines crafted from a dizzying number of grapes. While this reality makes for a terrific selection of delicious wines, it also makes understanding this state's wine regions—and knowing what to pick— challenging. Many wine books divide California into four major areas, but that's not necessarily

CALIFORNIA

helpful for the everyday buyer. After all, within these broad divisions lie dozens of appellations— American Viticultural Areas, or AVAs, in technical parlance. (Fun fact: the first American AVA was created in Missouri.)

An AVA is a specific, delimited growing area identified by its unique combination of soil and climate. AVAs can overlap, or one can be located within another. Some are well known, others not so much. Not all designations are AVAs: areas with political boundaries, such as the name of a county, don't need official certification; they can just use their regional name without any other rigmarole. So, is there a way to summarize a state with over 107 AVAs, 100 grape varietals, and seemingly innumerable wine styles? You bet! Strap in and let's go!

SANTA BARBARA

What You Need to Know

This area is home to a broad array of good to excellent wines, and a great source for everyday sippers.

Grapes

Pinot noir and chardonnay are the primary grapes, particularly in the cooler coastal areas. The warmer inland sections are home to cabernet, grenache, syrah, viognier, and sauvignon blanc. In addition, a small but ever-increasing number of producers there make excellent wines from traditional Italian varietals such as sangiovese, barbera, pinot grigio, and arneis, the trend known as Cali-Itali.

What to Look For

Fans of cool-climate pinot and chardonnay should look for wines from the Santa Maria Valley or Sta. Rita Hills. These wines are almost burgundian in their lean minerality yet still have the undeniable California fruitiness. The Santa Ynez Valley straddles the warm/cool divide and is thus a good source for cabernet, merlot, pinot noir, and the Rhône varietals. Regardless of which appellation wines are from, they are known for their concentrated flavor. Happy Canyon of Santa Barbara and Ballard Canyon are warmer climates perfect for the alternate varietals including cabernet, syrah, sauvignon blanc, and viogner, among others. These wines are equally flavorful but have a richer, fuller feel on the palate.

More Details

The mountains that stretch along the west coast of the Americas generally run north-south, as one would expect. However, there is a curious fifty-mile stretch in Santa Barbara County where the mountains make a ninety-degree turn. This geographical quirk creates a unique east-west traverse that allows the cool Pacific air to infiltrate the region and its AVAs. The changes in air temperature create numerous microclimates that allow its array of wine grapes to thrive. In addition, it makes Santa Barbara one of the coolest growing areas in California.

What You Need to Know

Think boutique, smaller production wines that combine the full flavors of California with a French wine's structure and finesse. The under-the-radar status of this region also makes these bottles a great value.

Grapes

Cabernet and merlot are the two most widely grown varietals. Chardonnay, pinot noir, syrah, and viognier are among the other twenty or so grapes grown here.

What to Look For

Vineyards in San Luis Obispo are situated, on average, just five miles from the Pacific, giving their wines their cool, crisp elegance. There are only four AVAs within this region. Edna Valley is home to top-notch chardonnay and pinot noir and is known for its unoaked white wines.

These wines in general are rich and juicy. (Spoiler: this is also a great appellation for bubbly!) The adjacent Arroyo Grande Valley encompasses both cool and warm climates. Good pinot noir and chardonnay are made in the cooler valleys, while the warmer elevations are home to petite syrah, syrah, viognier, and zinfandel. Expect these wines to be full and rich. The largest and warmest appellation in this region is Paso Robles, the perfect spot for producing cabernet, syrah, and zinfandel. These wines are full-flavored, luscious, and big. Finally, there is York Mountain, notable for being home to York Mountain Winery. Founded in 1882 as Ascension Winery, it has the distinction of being the first winery on California's Central Coast and one of the oldest continuously operating wineries in the US. These wines—generally pinot noir, cabernet, or syrah—are very concentrated and lush.

More Details

Though grapes were planted in San Luis Obispo back in the days of the Spanish missions, this region's modern wine history is barely thirty years old. Known for its intimacy, it is now home to a relatively small number of boutique wineries. Perhaps as a result of its youth, the majority of San Luis Obispo's vineyards are Sustainability in Practice (SIP) certified. These growers focus on the whole farm system approach, encompassing everything from water and habitat conservation to social responsibility, energy efficiency to pest management, as a way to protect their natural and human resources.

What You Need to Know

This area was once home to a small number of producers churning out large quantities of wine. (Paul Masson was one of this area's pioneers.) Today the ratio is reversed, and the area hosts numerous small estates producing some very interesting wines.

Grapes

Chardonnay dominates here, though riesling, pinot noir, cabernet, and merlot are also quite popular.

What to Look For

If you like pinot noir and chardonnay, look for wines from Arroyo Seco (which will have lots of tropical fruit flavor), Chalone (floral and minerally), or Santa Lucia Highlands (intense fruit with subtler minerality.) For warmer-climate wines made with cabernet or merlot, look for wines from the Carmel Valley, Hames Valley, or San Antonio Valley.

More Details

The most distinctive geographical feature of Monterey County is actually underwater. The Blue Grand Canyon is a sixty-mile-long, two-mile-deep canyon that is unnaturally close to the shoreline of Monterey Bay. This deep, cold water gives the area its fog, wind, and moderate temperatures and has the curious effect of limiting rain during growing season. Because of this influence, there is a forty-degree temperature difference between the inland vineyards and those closest to the bay.

What You Need to Know

This is California's most prolific wine area, producing nearly equal amounts of red and white wine.

Grapes

Chardonnay, merlot, and cabernet sauvignon are the most widely planted varietals, but some thirty other grapes grow in Sonoma. Interestingly, more pinot noir is grown here than anywhere else in the state.

What to Look For

Sonoma's six fertile valleys run the gamut from cool to warm climate, making it home to an array of grapes that produce some truly distinctive wines. If you're a fan of ripe, flavorful wines made from chardonnay, cabernet, merlot, and other warm-weather-loving grapes, look for bottles from the Alexander Valley, Sonoma Mountain, or Knights Valley. Some of the best zinfandels come from the warmer Dry Creek Valley and Rockpile appellations. With vines planted there for more than 130 years, Dry Creek is also a go-to spot for old vine zinfandel. For crisp, flavorful chardonnay and pinot noir from cooler climates, look for wines from the Russian River Valley, Sonoma Valley, Carneros, or Sonoma Coast. The Sonoma Coast is also a great source for syrah, while Carneros is known for its bubbly. Finally, white wine lovers should seek out zippy, minerally chardonnay and sauvignon blanc from Chalk Hill.

More Details

Sonoma is the birthplace of California agriculture and has long been recognized as a top spot for winegrowing. For example, it was a coveted post for the early Spanish missionaries—but not because it offered better weather or a good work environment. Instead, it was because Sonoma's mission had the best sacramental wine. Subsequently, Russian colonists planted vines there in 1812, but they weren't the European varietals we know and love today. It was the self-styled Count Agoston Haraszthy who kicked off Sonoma's modern wine era. In 1855, he brought more than 100,000 vines from Europe—including cabernet, chardonnay, and other common varietals—and established the Buena Vista Winery. While Prohibition was a commercial failure for Sonoma—the number of wineries declined from 256 to less than fifty in thirteen years—the industry continued to thrive thanks to a loophole allowing home winemaking. As a result, it is suspected that grape acreage actually increased during this time, as did overall alcohol consumption.

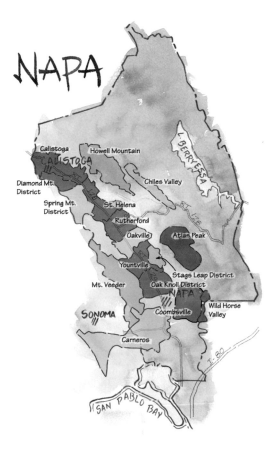

What You Need to Know

Two words are all you need to know about this region: cabernet sauvignon. Napa stands as one of the best wine regions in the world, thanks to a superb growing environment for this red grape.

Grapes

Cabernet dominates this region, with nearly double the acreage of the area's second most widely planted grape, chardonnay. But you can find other Bordeaux varietals growing there, most notably merlot and cabernet franc, as well as zinfandel, sauvignon blanc, and a smattering of other grapes.

What to Look For

Cabernet, of course! Cabs from cooler areas tend to present in an Old World style: earthy, leaner, and more tannic. If that's your cup of tea, seek out wines from Atlas Peak, Carneros, Howell Mountain, Oak Knoll, Wild Horse Valley, and Yountville. Those from warmer appellations are generally New World in style, so think lush, forward, and fruity. Look for Calistoga, Diamond Mountain, Oakville, Rutherford, St. Helena, or Stags Leap on the label. Of course, several appellations straddle these extremes, producing wines that can have the best of both worlds. These areas with more moderate temperatures include Coombsville, Mt. Veeder, and Spring Mountain District. And while the obvious answer is cabernet, don't ignore the other delicious wines that come from this great region. Zinfandel fans can find some good ones from Atlas Peak, Calistoga, and St. Helena. Merlot purists can find nice versions from Calistoga, Oak Knoll District, Oakville, Rutherford, or Spring Mountain. Carneros, again, makes a good source for bubbly. Yes, I did just mention Carneros in the previous section. So glad you noticed. The appellation straddles both Napa and Sonoma, so both larger regions get to claim it as theirs.

Finally, I would be remiss for not mentioning a wine style called Meritage.

This is Napa's answer to the Bordeaux blend—a wine made from a combination of cabernet, merlot, cabernet franc, malbec, petit verdot, and/or carménère (carmen-air) grapes. (Hint: cab and merlot are the most commonly used!) However, under federal regulations, such a wine would have to be labeled as "red table wine." For the winemakers handcrafting these high-end wines, that simply wouldn't do, so in 1988 they formed an alliance and held a contest to come up with a sophisticated name that could be used on the labels of these wines.

The winner?

Meritage—a combination of "merit" and "heritage" that rhymes with the latter. (Don't worry if you've been mispronouncing it: most people do, including me for many years!)

More Details

George Yount was the first person to plant vines in Napa in 1839, in present-day Yountville. The first commercial winery wasn't established for another twenty-two years, though growth after that came quickly. By 1889, there were 140 wineries in the valley, including Schramsberg, Beringer, and Inglenook—names that are still around today. Prohibition decimated the industry (surprise!), and it wasn't until the 1960s that Napa reestablished itself as a wine region, becoming a dominant player on the world wine stage in relatively short order. Today, even though it is just one-eighth the size of Bordeaux, Napa stands next to this renowned area as one of the top wine-producing regions in the world.

The Central Valley

What You Need to Know

This region produces nearly 75 percent of California's wine grapes, but most wine production is of the bulk variety.

Grapes

Chardonnay, zinfandel, and French colombard are the most widely planted grapes.

What to Look For

Zinfandel from Lodi, the region's best-known AVA, is a standout for one simple reason: 40 percent of California's premium zinfandel wine is made there. Whether dubbed "old vine," "zinfandel," or just "zin," these wines offer terrific fruity, jammy, juicy flavor; go well with food; and give good bang for the buck.

More Details

Traditionally, most of the grapes grown there are used for bulk wine or are shipped elsewhere for blending purposes. Even though the area has seventeen AVAs, many of them have just one or two wineries, making the bottles hard to find at wine shops. Zin first came to America in the early 1800s and migrated west with the 49ers during the gold rush. While no vines from that initial wave have survived, zinfandel vines from as far back as the 1880s are still producing small quantities of fruit.

At this point, you might be asking: What's the deal with old vine zinfandel?

These vines are believed to have been planted in the late 1800s and are part of Sonoma's Morelli Lane Vineyard; Dutton-Goldfield Winery buys these grapes for their wine.

Think of grapevines as people. Babies aren't very interesting, which changes, of course, as they age. Think about it: the oldest person in the room is often the one with the best stories to tell. And so it is with grapevines. Once planted, it takes about four years for the fruit to be mature enough to make into wine. But as the vine continues to grow, the wines gain more depth, character, and flavor with each vintage. Though there is no standard definition of an "old vine," it is generally considered to be one that is fifty or more years old. Ancient vines are generally eighty-plus years old.

Further, zinfandel has a near monopoly on wines with old vine status. Most other grapevines hit their peak sometime between the ages of thirty and fifty, with fruit quality declining from there. Zin is one of the few varietals whose quality improves beyond these years.

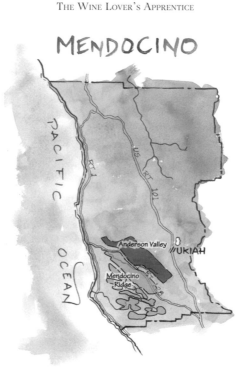

What You Need to Know

A lot of hidden gems lurk within this region, but your best bet is its sparkling wine.

Grapes

Lots of terrific chardonnay and cabernet sauvignon are made here, but the region is home to virtually all of the one hundred-plus varietals grown in California. Also popular are zinfandel, pinot noir, syrah, and sauvignon blanc.

What to Look For

The aforementioned bubbly from Anderson Valley is a crisp, fresh wine that can stand shoulder-to-shoulder with the best from Champagne. Zinfandel wines from Mendocino Ridge have been described as "seductive monsters." They can be hard to find but are worth seeking out if you like big, bold, and juicy. (Trivia: Mendocino Ridge is the only non-contiguous AVA in the US. It covers a series of coastal ridges above 1,200 feet but does not include their connecting valleys.)

More Details

If San Luis Obispo has cornered the market on Sustainability in Practice (SIP), Mendocino county is California's organic wine Mecca. In part, this is because the area is all about family farms, with the second and third generations still living on and farming the land settled by their forebears. As a result, more than 25 percent of the county's grapes are organically or biodynamically farmed. Organic farming, of course, eschews the use of artificial pesticides, fertilizers, and other such treatments. Biodynamic farming combines these ecological principles with spiritual elements—such as planting vines and harvesting grapes based on the phases of the moon—to create a holistic approach to farming. If 25 percent doesn't sound like a lot, consider this number: one-third of the organic wine grape acreage in California is found in Mendocino. And, don't you know, these grapes are also GMO-free.

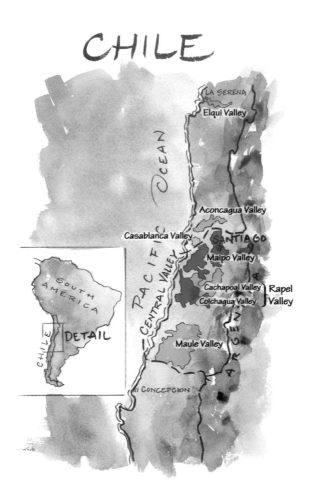

Chile

Conquistadors planted the first grapes in Chile back in 1551. That varietal—pais, or mission, as it was called in the US—was the country's most widely planted grape until the 21st century. That's when it was displaced by cabernet sauvignon. But that's not the country's most important grape, either. Nope, the varietal that Chile claims as its official grape is . . . carménère. This is an ancient varietal that once grew alongside cabernet and merlot in Bordeaux's vineyards. These three grapes (among others) made their way from France to Chile in the early 1800s, when it became chic for the country's upper classes to travel abroad. Needless to say, the locals developed quite the taste for French wine, and clever entrepreneurs began importing and planting French grapevines to capture this market.

Two interesting things happened along the way.

First, when the grapes were brought over, growers and vintners confused the carménère grapes for merlot. This was an understandable mistake, as the grapes share a similar color and leaf shape. It wasn't until 1994 that DNA research showed that the grape believed to be a merlot clone was actually carménère. Given that the carménère grape is virtually extinct in France, this discovery caused quite a stir, giving the grape new life, and offering Chile a way to break into the global wine marketplace.

Carménère's extinction in France dates back to the 1880s, when the phylloxera louse destroyed a significant portion of the country's vineyards. (This pest attacks and damages vines at the roots, a problem typically solved by regrafting vines onto American rootstock, which is resistant to the louse.) Which brings us to the second interesting event in the country's wine history.

By a stroke of luck, the French vines brought to Chile in the 19th century left the country before the phylloxera epidemic struck, which means that all the vines in Chile grow on their original rootstocks. As a result, many experts suggest that these vines produce wines that are more "authentic," with a taste more similar to French wines of the 1800s than the French wines of today. (Others say a wine's flavors are due to the environment and winemaker, with the roots contributing little or nothing to the wine's flavor.)

Modernization is the buzzword in Chile today, and the country's winemakers delight in pushing the envelope. They have planted vines at some of the highest elevations and coolest climates in the world. Vintages vary little from year to year since most of Chile has very consistent weather, with almost no risk of summer frost or rain at harvest, which is between February and April in the southern hemisphere. Casablanca, Chile's fastest growing wine region, is the exception due to its proximity to the Pacific Ocean.

Aconcagua Region

What You Need to Know

Aconcagua is a good area for both value and high-end wines.

Grapes

Numerous grapes are grown here, including cabernet sauvignon, syrah, carménère, and pinot noir for reds, and chardonnay and sauvignon blanc for whites.

What to Look For

There are two major winegrowing valleys in this area. First is the namesake Aconcagua Valley. This is the go-to spot in Chile for red wines, despite the seemingly inhospitable hot, dry climate. Cabernets dominate, but, as a whole, these reds are generally quite strong, full, and fruity. The area's winemakers have discovered that the coast is a great spot for sauvignon blanc, making them hidden gems—that is, at least until the rest of the wine world catches on! The other subregion to know about is the Casablanca Valley. Primarily a white wine region, the cool climate means plantings of pinot noir are increasing rapidly! Vines were first planted here in the 1980s, making it the youngest significant wine region in Chile. The winemakers achieved a rapid rise in the global wine market by focusing on quality, not quantity. Both red and white wines from the Casablanca Valley are quite crisp and fresh with lots of great fruit flavor.

Wine Flavors

It is easy to assume that the wines we drink today taste similar to the wines people drank eighty, one hundred, and even 150 years ago. Surprise—they don't! In fact, a wine's flavors and style can change significantly over time, for reasons ranging from advancements in winemaking to changes in taste buds. For example, Bordeaux wines of the 1600s were very light and thin, nothing like the full, tannic wines we drink today. Chianti is another great example: hundreds of years ago, this savory red wine actually used to be white. Eventually, the blend changed to include some red grapes, with the proportion of white grapes ever-decreasing. Today's version is made exclusively with red grapes. Even Chile isn't immune. In the 1600s, the country's wines were oxidized and vinegary. A century later, tastes dictated sweet wines. And a wine writer of the 19th century described Chilean wine as a "potion of rhubarb and senna," the latter a flowering plant with a slightly bitter taste. I'm guessing he wasn't a fan.

Central Valley

What You Need to Know

The Central Valley is the most productive and best-known wine region in Chile due largely to its proximity to Santiago. Coincidentally, it is directly across the Andes from Argentina's Mendoza region.

Grapes

The top four grapes are cabernet, carménère, sauvignon blanc, and chardonnay.

What to Look For

For the most part, the Central Valley is home to red wine production, but good value whites can be found there too. Several subregions are worth noting. The Maipo, Rapel, and Cachapoal (catch-a-poe-al) Valleys are red wine country. These areas are good sources for bold and full-bodied cabernet and carménère. White wine lovers can look to the Maipo Valley as a good source for flavorful, citrusy sauvignon blanc. The Colchagua Valley— considered Chile's answer to Napa—is great for an array of full-bodied reds, from cabernet and carménère to syrah and malbec as well as crisp, clean white wines. The true value spot, however, is the Maule Valley. Winemakers here turned their focus to quality production in the 1990s and today are making some terrifically powerful cabernets alongside aromatic, spicy carménère wines.

FRANCE

ENGLISH CHANNEL

BELGIUM

GERMANY

PARIS

Champagne

SWITZ.

Loire Valley

BAY of BISCAY

Burgundy

Beaujolais

Bordeaux

Rhône Valley

ITALY

Languedoc-
Roussillon

Provence

MARSEILLE

SPAIN

Corsica

MEDITERRANEAN SEA

France

It's hard not to feel intimidated by French wines. I get it. Looking at some French wine labels is an exercise in staring blankly. Château blah blah? Clos something-or-other? What the heck is a cru? Can I get a translator over here?

To be fair, the French convention of labeling wine by its region came about hundreds of years ago. Even as recently as the 1970s, American winemakers labeled their wines "Chablis" or "Burgundy" because that's what the public understood to be white and red wine, regardless of the actual grape contained therein. Unfortunately, that strategy leaves out the fact that red Bordeaux is typically a cabernet sauvignon-merlot blend, or that sancerre is made with sauvignon blanc in the Loire Valley. (Um, where?) The country's appellation system doesn't necessarily help much: in addition to the three broad, national appellations (reduced from four in 2012), many regions layer on their own ranking systems. We'll deal with those in the individual sections, but it's worth a quick look at the three national classifications:

Vin de France indicates a table wine and shows the grape(s) and vintage on the label. These are generally fairly simple wines for early drinking. The intermediate level is Indication Géographique Protégée, which indicates grape, vintage, and region on the label. The uppermost level is Appellation d'Origine Protégée (AOP), formerly Appellation d'Origine Contrôlée (AOC). Though the name changed, the very strict standards are the same. As such, these categories can serve as a rough guideline to quality. However, there is another fairly easy way to navigate a French wine label: the more specific the information, the better quality the wine is likely to be. A wine labeled "Bourgogne" (the broad region) will be more basic than a wine labeled "Charmes-Chambertin" (a specific commune), which will be more interesting than the Bourgogne but less so than a wine with "Clos Vougeot" (a vineyard) on the label. Choosing a wine using this strategy is not fail-safe, but it's a good guideline to use for one not well versed in the ins and outs of Burgundy wines (or Bordeaux or, really, a lot of other regions, French or non). And with that, let's get to the many regions of this wine-prolific country.

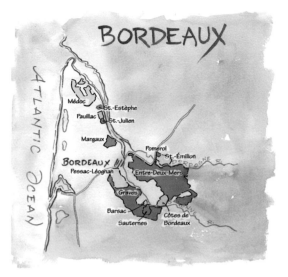

What You Need to Know

These wines are hailed as some of the best in the world. However, they can also seem highly overrated if their style doesn't suit your palate.

Grapes

Cabernet sauvignon and merlot are the primary red grapes grown there. Cabernet franc, petit verdot, and malbec are grown in much smaller quantities. Single varietal red wines are rarely produced; most Bordeaux are blends of the above grapes. White wines from Bordeaux are made from sauvignon blanc and sémillon, also usually blended.

What to Look For

Bordeaux is divided by the Gironde River, and the best estates are lined along the left and right banks of the river, intuitively referred to as the "Left Bank" and "Right Bank."

The left bank has heavy clay soil more suited to cabernet sauvignon, so these wines tend to have the largest proportion of cabernet in the blends. They are dark and concentrated, showing notes of blackberry, dark cherry, vanilla, coffee, and spice. The best appellations are St.-Estèphe, Pauillac, St.-Julien, and Margaux.

Merlot dominates the wines crafted on the right bank. As a result, they tend to be rounder and more elegant than their cabernet-based counterparts. While they often show the same dark fruit qualities, the flavors are leavened with notes of plum, chocolate, and blueberry jam. Appellations to look for are St-Émilion and Pomerol. Wines from both of these areas tend to be costly, as they are home to some of the best châteaux and have considerable name recognition. For value reds, look to lesser-known regions like the Côtes de Bordeaux, Médoc, Graves, and the four St.-Émilion satellites—they go by (Name)-St-Émilion. These blends may lack the richness and longevity of their more expensive counterparts, but they can still offer wonderful layers of flavor and nuance at more budget-friendly prices.

Now let's turn our attention to white wines, a style most people, understandably, don't associate with Bordeaux. However, that lack of recognition also makes them hidden (if occasionally pricey) gems. The best dry white wines are from Pessac-Léognan. Ranging in style from deep and concentrated to minerally and refreshing, these wines are blends of sauvignon blanc and sémillon. Typical flavors include lemon, flowers, spice, honey, butter, and vanilla. Similar versions can be found at more everyday prices from the Entre-Deux-Mers region. The same two grapes in these dry wines are also responsible for some of the world's best dessert wines. From the regions of Sauternes (the best) and Barsac (the value), these wines are full of honeyed richness disguised in tropical fruit flavors. Don't worry about the sweetness: these wines have enough acidity to cut through the sugar, making them luscious, as opposed to candy flavored.

More Details

While it is getting easier to find good Bordeaux at value prices, this is still a region where you don't want to skimp. (Many a drinker has wondered what the fuss is about after tasting a really lousy ten-dollar Bordeaux.) Unless you have a source who can direct you to a good, inexpensive version, it's best to pony up when buying these wines. You should be willing to spend about thirty dollars and up at a retail store and closer to sixty dollars and up at a restaurant. Another option is to look for second labels—wines from well-known châteaux that offer great quality without the hefty price tag of their more prestigious first label. These creations use fruit that didn't quite make the cut for the most expensive bottlings. Rather than waste or try to sell the fruit, winemakers created these "lesser" wines to expand their market, a win-win for the winery and wine drinker on a budget. To give you an idea of how much you would save when buying a second label, a bottle of 2009 Château Latour will run you at least $1,600. The same vintage of Les Forts de Latour is a comparatively mere $250. (Don't worry—most second labels can be had for much less!)

The 1855 Classification: Who Needs It Anyway?

Much ado is made about the 1855 classification of Bordeaux wines, which was an attempt at both snobbishness and marketing. Emperor Napoleon III requested this ranking to showcase the country's best Bordeaux wines for international visitors at the 1855 Exposition Universelle de Paris. The ranking was based largely on price and has since had only two changes: the addition of Cantemerle in 1856, perhaps left off as an oversight; and the promotion in 1973 of Mouton-Rothschild to first-growth status, after much lobbying from the Rothschild family. In the meantime, though, winemaking and the region have changed significantly. While the first growths remain some of the best wines in the world, many estates today are better—or worse—than their rank. Further, many excellent wines are left out of the classification entirely. Bottom line? Feel free to ignore it.

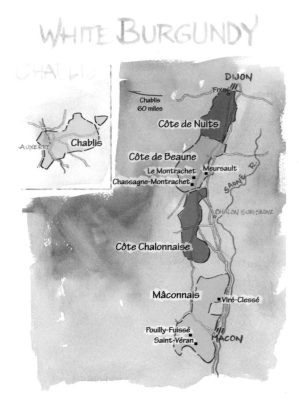

What You Need to Know

Burgundy wines are deliciously drinkable and among the most food-friendly available. If you're going out to eat and aren't sure what to order, head for this section of the wine list. However, these wines can be pricey—and vintage important—so order judiciously and ask for a recommendation from the sommelier or wine store manager if you're going high end.

Grapes

Pinot noir and chardonnay predominate this region. *
other grapes can be found here, the most notable being gamay from the
Beaujolais region.

What to Look For

For all its villages, double-barreled names, and premier and grand cru
sites, picking a wine from Burgundy is actually pretty simple. (Premier
cru and grand cru are classifications, essentially meaning second and first
best, respectively. In Burgundy, the designations are given to vineyards.)
If it's a white wine, it's chardonnay; if it's a red wine, it's pinot noir. But
the devil, as they say, is in the details.

Let's start with white wines first, heading from areas in the region
north to south. Chablis (sha-blee) is probably the best known of the
region's stellar white wines. Once part of Champagne, this region's wines
(which are still—not bubbly) are steely and racy with a bracing acidity
and minerally spine. This area is a source for both high-end and value
wines. The other great area for white wine is Côte de Beaune, home to
numerous villages producing some of the best chardonnay in the world.
Le Montrachet (only the second "t" is silent) is hands down the greatest of these, with the price tag to match. Various other wines have the
Montrachet name attached, which are also worth seeking out. Regardless
of origin, these wines lean toward complex, layered flavors with minerally
backbones. If (not overbearing) rich and buttery is more your style, try
wines from Meursault or Chassagne-Montrachet. If you're looking for
value chardonnay, the Mâconnais region is your go-to. Wines from this
broad appellation are delicious, but you can look for some of the village
wines, as well. The best of these include Pouilly-Fuissé, Saint-Véran, and
Viré-Clessé. These wines come in a range of styles, but expect to find
crisp, easygoing wines that are a pleasure to drink.

Funny enough, Burgundy's red wines make a similar north to south
progression, with the best wines from the cooler regions and the value
wines found closer to the Mediterranean.

Taking it from the top: The Côte de Nuits (silent "s") is home to
some of the best pinot noir wines in the world. Big, earthy versions can
be found from the villages of Gevrey-Chambertin and Morey-St-Denis.

RED BURGUNDY

For a lighter style, seek out wines from Chambolle-Musigny, Vougeot (voo-zho), or Vosne-Romanée (vone ro-man-nay). For value, grab an earthy-style red from the village of Fixin. Ironically, the Côte de Beaune's reputation for white wine makes it a good place to find value pinot! Look for earthy styles from Pommard and lighter, more elegant versions from Savigny-lès-Beaune (sav-ee-nyee) and Volnay. For even better value (but perhaps less nuance in the glass), the Côte Chalonnaise is the place to look. You'll want a bottle from Givry (ghee-vree) or Mercurey, whose full-bodied wines were allegedly a favorite of Gabrielle d'Estrées, mistress of King Henry IV of France, who apparently preferred the light, lithe Givry pinots.

BEAUJOLAIS

Finally, we come to the southernmost part of Burgundy and a place that is technically part of Burgundy (hence its inclusion here) but with wines unlike anything else in that region or, really, the world. This area made its reputation back in the 1980s on a little drink called Beaujolais Nouveau, a fruity trifle of a wine that was crafted for its drinkability and invades wine stores every November. But, like the relationship between Beaujolais and Burgundy, the nouveau wine bears little resemblance to its more sophisticated counterparts. The red grape gamay rules in Beaujolais and, in the right hands, becomes a juicy, savory wine that goes brilliantly with food. Forget the nouveau and grab a bottle from one of the ten cru Beaujolais areas: Brouilly, Régnié, Chiroubles, Côte de Brouilly, Fleurie, St.-Amour, Chénas, Juliénas, Morgon, and Moulin-à-Vent.

These wines vary in style and are listed from lightest to heaviest. Primary flavors include cranberry and raspberry highlighted with notes of earth, smoke, or purple flowers. Delicious anytime, these wines are particularly delightful when served slightly chilled at a summer barbeque.

Champagne

What You Need to Know

Perfect for celebrations, Champagne makes for a surprising everyday choice to pair with lobster, sushi, and spicy Asian cuisine.

Grapes

Most Champagne is made of a blend of pinot noir, chardonnay, and/ or pinot meunier. A blanc de blancs is made solely from chardonnay; a blanc de noirs is crafted exclusively from pinot noir or, more rarely, pinot meunier—and sometimes both.

What to Look For

An executive at Veuve Clicquot once told me that vintage Champagne offers a better value than either nonvintage (NV) or prestige bottles such as La Grande Dame, Dom Pérignon, or Comtes de Champagne. Why? Unlike the NV, vintage Champagne is made only in the best years of grape production. Pricewise, it often costs much less than the prestige cuvées, and not much more than your basic bubbly from this area, putting them in the sweet spot for quality and value.

More Details

All Champagne is sparkling wine, but not all sparkling wine is Champagne. Under French wine laws, two criteria must be met in order to call bubbly wine Champagne. First, the wine must be produced in the Champagne region of northern France. Next, the secondary fermentation that gives the wine its bubbles must take place

Champagne in the middle of riddling, the process of moving sediment into the neck so it can be removed before the bottle is properly corked.

in the bottle in which the sparkler is eventually sold.

The classic Champagne style is nonvintage. Its creation is a truly impressive feat: the wine is a blend of different grapes taken from various vineyards during several harvests. Accomplishing this act of chemistry requires great skill, as the winemaker has to combine as many as seventy different base wines (which constantly evolve) into a house-style cuvée that tastes the same—or at least very similar— year after year. One of the most notable things about Champagne is that it is ready for drinking upon release. And, though some can be aged for years, most should be enjoyed within the first year or so of purchase.

LANGUEDOC-ROUSSILLON/PROVENCE

Languedoc-Roussillon

What You Need to Know

Red and white wines from here tend to make great everyday drinking wines.

Grapes

A whole mish-mosh of grapes grow here. French varietals include mourvèdre, grenache, syrah, and viognier (the white grape in this list), while the international merlot, cabernet sauvignon, sauvignon blanc, and chardonnay grapes are also popular.

What to Look For

Languedoc reds tend to be strong and elegant with a rustic tone. Look for wines from the appellations of Corbières, Fitou, Faugères, or Minervois, which tend to be the smoothest from this region. Benedictine monks at Saint-Hilaire were crafting sparkling wine some

87

150 years before the Champenois. Look for wines from the Limoux (lee-moo), Blanquette de Limoux, or Crémant de Limoux appellations. The dry wine appellations in Roussillon (Roo-see-yone) are Côtes du Roussillon, Collioure, and Côtes du Roussillon-Villages. These wines tend to be richly flavored and generously fruity. For gobsmackingly delicious dark and rustic dessert wines (if that's your thing), look for the Banyuls or Maury appellations. A word to the wise: these are a perfect accompaniment to chocolate.

Provence

What You Need to Know

Provence is all about the pink!

Grapes

The primary grapes found here include grenache, syrah, and mourvèdre, though other local grapes are often blended into these wines.

What to Look For

Contrary to many people's impression of rosé, pink wine from Provence is fresh, crisp, bright, and dry. This wine is extremely versatile with food and delightful just to sip. Though vast improvements have been made to the quality of pink wine, it can still be hit or miss. Bandol is considered the best appellation in the region. Many good wines also come from the Coteaux Varois and Coteaux d'Aix-en-Provence appellations. Look for a familiar producer from this area to avoid a miss. Les Baux-de-Provence is an interesting region, since all vineyards are required to be farmed bio-dynamically.

More Details

People tend to think of rosés as sweet wines, which makes sense if they drink American blush wine a.k.a. white zinfandel. Putting that notion to rest, American blush wines contain nearly seven times the residual sugar per liter—what's left after fermentation—as a pink wine from Provence!

What You Need to Know

Wines from this region are super food-friendly, though they can be pricey despite their lack of name recognition.

Grapes

The primary white grapes grown here are chenin blanc, muscadet, and sauvignon blanc, while the main red grape is cabernet franc.

What to Look For

The Loire Valley stretches from the Atlantic Ocean halfway across France, a distance of 630 miles. You'd think that familiarizing yourself with such a vast wine region would be difficult, but it's actually pretty easy. First up is muscadet. This name is used for both the grape and the white wine it produces. Muscadet grows primarily in the region of Pays Nantes, which is nestled against the Atlantic Ocean. Hints of the sea infuse the wine as a result. Overall, these light-bodied wines are bracing and crisp with flavors of apple and citrus. As you might imagine, this wine goes brilliantly with oysters and shellfish. The Sèvre-et-Main appellation is considered the best for producing richer, more flavorful wines. Sticking with white wines, let's look at chenin blanc. Wines from this grape can be very intense, with notes of straw, quince, chamomile, and even a bit of honey. Savennières and Vouvray are two of the best regions for these wines. It's worth noting that Loire Valley chenin blanc is crafted in a variety of styles, from sweet to bone-dry, still and sparkling, and everything in between. You honestly can't go wrong with any of them, so go with what your taste buds are craving. The third major white grape in the Loire is sauvignon blanc. These are not the blowsy, exuberant wines most think of when referring to this grape. Instead, this style of sauvignon is much more restrained and elegant, with floral and spice notes as well as a hint of minerality. The best of them are from Sancerre and Pouilly Fumé, which have a distinct, smoky character. Look to Touraine to find these wines on a budget.

Finally, for reds, cabernet franc is the undisputed champ. Some of the best selections come from Saumur-Champigny and Chinon. Both wines tend to be light to medium bodied, with savory flavors of spice, violets, and berries. For a fuller wine with silky notes of spice and fruit, seek one out from Bourgueil (boor-guy-uh).

RHÔNE VALLEY

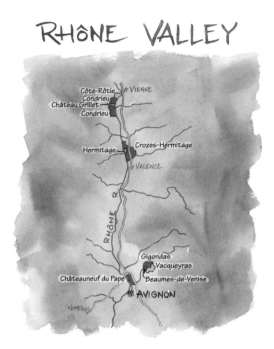

What You Need to Know

This region is known for spicy, fiery red wines. Think matching with food, not sipping, when choosing wines from the Rhône!

Grapes

Though numerous varietals are cultivated here, the primary grapes are viognier (white), syrah, and grenache (both red).

What to Look For

The Rhône divides easily into two regions. Northern Rhône is syrah country, where the grape makes up all or most of the wine. The best quality regions are Côte-Rotie and Hermitage (silent "h"), where the wines are dense and dark. Crozes-Hermitage makes a good alternative to the pricier reds. Lovely dry white wines from the viognier grape are made in the Condrieu and Château Grillet (gree-ay) appellations. The latter are a little less perfumed and hedonistic—but longer-lived—than the former. From either appellation, these wines can be pricey but worth it. Conversely, the rule in the Southern Rhône is blend, blend, blend! Grenache is the dominant grape, though up to twelve other varietals are allowed in the wine. The best-known appellation in this region is Châteauneuf du Pape. Other areas to seek out include Vacqueyras and the very underrated Gigondas (zhi-gon-dahs). The generic appellation name is Côtes du Rhône, but bypass these wines in favor of a more specifically labeled Côtes du Rhône Villages (Village Name). These wines have stricter growing requirements but aren't AOC-level regions. Expect dark fruit and spice notes, with characteristic herbal flavors. They are lush and juicy, with a playfulness that contrasts to the elegance of their northern counterparts. Finally, the Rhône is also known for Muscat de Beaumes-de-Venise, a fortified sweet wine that has been made there since the 14th century. Today's version is honeyed with notes of tropical fruit.

ITALY

Lombardy

Veneto

Piedmont

Liguria

Tuscany

ADRIATIC SEA

ROME

Campania

TYRRHENIAN SEA

Basilicata

Sardinia

SICILY

Italy

Italy has a fantastically long winemaking history. There is fossil evidence of vitis vinifera—ancestors of today's noble grapes—dating back to pre-historic times. The Greeks brought grape vines to southern Italy in the 8th century BC, and the Etruscans made and traded wine from their kingdom in modern-day Tuscany. The Romans took these traditions and spread them far and wide. As a result, wine was one of the Romans' most important commodities from the 11th to 14th centuries. It was during this era that some of Italy's most famous wine families (think Frescobaldi and Antinori) established their estates. However, winemaking in Italy became a little too easy. Fast-forward to the 20th century, and the unfortunate results were clear: Italy was known for cheap, gimmicky wine with little flavor and even less character.

Things started to change in the 1960s (a really good decade for the wine industry overall), and today Italy has reemerged as a powerhouse, providing wines delightful for everyday drinking as well as big, flavorful, age-worthy wines that rank among the best in the world. Italy's appellation system now mirrors much of Europe's. The Vini and Vini Varietali designations indicate generic wines, the latter of which must contain at least 85 percent of an international varietal such as cabernet, merlot, or chardonnay. At the intermediate level, winemakers can use either Indicazione Geografica Tipica (IGT) or, less commonly, Vini Indicazione Geografica Protetta (IGP) on a wine label. These wines come from a specific territory with stricter regulations. Finally, Vini Denominazione di Origine Protetta (DOP) indicates the highest level of quality and is split into two levels: Denominazione di Origine Controllata (DOC) and Denominazione di Origine Controllata Garantita (DOCG), both with even more rigid regulations. But wait, there's more! A DOC or DOCG wine may also have "classico" or "superiore" on the label. Both terms indicate stricter requirements from the baseline levels. In addition, classico wines are from the area considered to be the heart of the DOC, while superiore wines have higher alcohol. A third term you might see on an Italian wine label is riserva, which indicates longer aging than a nonriserva wine.

Got all that? Good.

Thankfully, you won't be quizzed later.

PIEDMONT

What You Need to Know

This region's Barolo and Barbaresco wines are among the best in the world. But Piedmont is also home to a wonderful array of white, red, and fizzy wines, so ignore these lesser-known creations at your own risk!

Grapes

Nebbiolo is the region's most renowned grape. The other red grapes grown there are barbera (bar-bear-uh) and dolcetto, and the primary white grape is arneis.

What to Look For

Barolo and Barbaresco are Piedmont's heavy hitters—with prices to match. Though both are crafted only with nebbiolo, the wines grow in slightly different terroirs with different aging requirements. Both wines show similar flavors, including notes of cherries and roses. But Barolo is a heavier, more tannic wine than the lighter, fruitier Barbaresco—thus their designations as the "king" and "queen" (respectively) of Piedmont. Vintages are of greater importance with these wines, so a little research will help you select the right one. Most benefit from several years of cellaring, though Barbaresco is certainly drinkable at a younger age. If the wine is young, be sure to decant it first. For a wine similar in character and flavor without the heft—or hefty price tag— look for nebbiolo from the Langhe district. These wines are earthy and complex, and drinkable at a much younger age. (The wine's age, not yours!)

If Barolo and Barbaresco are "fancy" wines, barbera and dolcetto are the casual ones, served comfortably at a barbeque or pizza dinner. Often lumped together, these wines are distinctly different, though both share an affinity with food and can taste harsh without it. Barbera is high in acidity and low in tannins, making it very easy to drink. There are lots of dark fruit flavors, with notes of spice and licorice. Look for ones from Alba or Asti. Dolcetto is similarly acidic to barbera, though it is also more tannic. Flavors veer toward dried fruit and licorice with a slightly nutty quality. Those from Alba are considered to be the best.

Piedmont isn't a region usually associated with white wines, but two deserve a mention. The first is made from arneis, the region's principal white grape. These wines are rich, floral, and full-bodied: a smooth alternative to chardonnay. This wine also shines with food. The best come from the Roero district, though ones from Langhe can also be lovely. Second is Moscato d'Asti, a softly fizzy white wine made from the muscat grape. These wines are slightly sweet and enjoyable as a refreshing aperitif or with fruity desserts. This wine, unlike its fizzier cousin Asti Spumante, carries DOCG status.

Switching back to red (but a dessert wine, so sensibly placed last!), there is brachetto, a slightly sweet, slightly sparkling red dessert wine made from the brachetto grape. This one is worth trying, even if you think the words "red," "fizzy," and "dessert wine" don't belong together. I say this for one reason: brachetto is a refreshing palate cleanser, as it lacks the heft of many sweeter dessert wines. It is lovely on its own but makes a nice foil to chocolate desserts. Look for one designated Brachetto d'Acqui. You can thank me later.

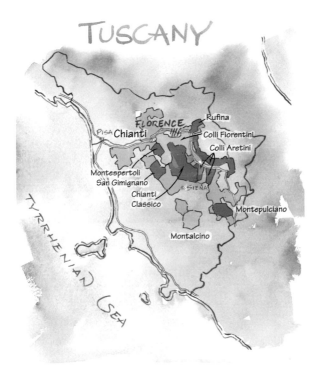

What You Need to Know

Most wine produced here is red, and most of that is crafted from the sangiovese grape. These wines are very food-friendly, but that shouldn't suggest they are simple in flavor.

Grapes

The white grapes cultivated in this region play a distant second fiddle to the reds. Sangiovese is the most important red grape, though a wide range of native and international varietals grow here, too.

What to Look For

The wine most associated with Tuscany is, of course, chianti. In general, these are medium-bodied, food-friendly wines that range from fruity and easy drinking to earthy and age-worthy. For those who like their wine on the lighter end of the spectrum, look for ones from Chianti (the overarching appellation) or its subzones of Colli Fiorentini and Colli Aretini. These are great choices to sip alone or enjoy with basic fare like pizza and pasta. Expect lots of fruity flavors, particularly the cherry, dark berry, and plum that are characteristic of the sangiovese grape. A riper, richer version of these wines can be found from Montespertoli, which was spun off from the Colli Fiorentini region in 1997 in recognition of its distinctive style.

Moving on to the fuller, more complex versions: Chianti Rufina is the region's only subzone that can truly rival chianti classico for its layered flavors and longevity. Rufina wines are light and elegant, bringing a lovely spicy-fruity quality to the table. In contrast, classico wines are powerful and firm, with notes of cherry and tomato and earthy undertones thrown in for good measure. These are wines to drink now, but the best can age for many years. Chianti classico wines may also have one of two other designations: Riserva, which indicates extra aging, and Gran Selezione, which has even stricter growing and aging requirements than those for the Classico designation. However, Chianti isn't the only game in town for red wines.

One of Italy's most revered wines is brunello di Montalcino (mon-tal-chee-no). It is made with a sangiovese clone that is unique to the region and gives the wine its sumptuous feel. These wines are big and opulent—you really want to drink this one around eight to ten years after the vintage—with flavors ranging from black fruits and leather to vanilla and spice. For an elegant version of this wine, go for a rosso di Montalcino. It spends less time in oak, so it comes across as lighter in texture, though the flavors are similar. Rosso di Montalcino can also be enjoyed at a much younger age—two to five years after the vintage. Vino nobile di Montepulciano is yet another sangiovese-based wine from another part of Tuscany, also with a fresher counterpart dubbed rosso di Montepulciano. These wines are more lithe and elegant, with red fruit and plum flavors. (By the way, don't confuse these wines with Montepulciano d'Abruzzo, a wine made from a different grape from a different region.) Finally, we get to Tuscany's white wine: Vernaccia di San Gimignano. This sipping wine—made with the vernaccia grape—is dry with a characteristic nutty finish.

More Details

Okay, so I've left off a category of wines known as "super Tuscans." The name doesn't honor some particularly heroic Etruscans of yore; instead, it was coined for marketing purposes. Here's what happened:

The country's wine laws don't leave much room for experimentation, so for years, winemakers who wanted to try something different (i.e., break the rules) had to label their wines as IGT even though they were top quality and fairly pricey. Eventually, these wines were dubbed superTuscan as a way to avoid the stigma and distinguish themselves from all of the ordinary IGT wines for sale. These wines may have sangiovese grapes in them but are also just as likely to contain only cabernet sauvignon or a cabernet/merlot blend or a combination of all three! The best known of these wines are Ornellaia, Tignanello, and Sassicaia, the latter of which was the first super-Tuscan released to the market back in 1971. Any of these three bottles will cost you three figures or more, but don't fret—many other excellent superTuscan wines can be readily found at lower prices.

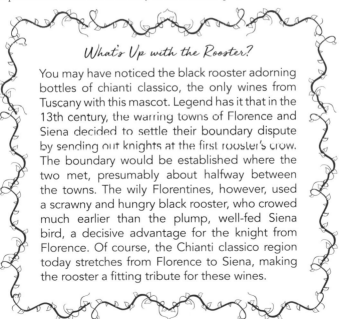

What's Up with the Rooster?

You may have noticed the black rooster adorning bottles of chianti classico, the only wines from Tuscany with this mascot. Legend has it that in the 13th century, the warring towns of Florence and Siena decided to settle their boundary dispute by sending out knights at the first rooster's crow. The boundary would be established where the two met, presumably about halfway between the towns. The wily Florentines, however, used a scrawny and hungry black rooster, who crowed much earlier than the plump, well-fed Siena bird, a decisive advantage for the knight from Florence. Of course, the Chianti classico region today stretches from Florence to Siena, making the rooster a fitting tribute for these wines.

VENETO

What You Need to Know

This region is known for some of the world's unique and most delicious wines but also produces good wine for everyday quaffers.

Grapes

The main red grapes are the native varietals corvina, molinara, and rondinello. White grapes include glera, garganega, and trebbiano.

What to Look For

Wines from the Prosecco region make an excellent start to a meal or just an evening with friends. They are made from the glera grape (formerly known as prosecco—the name change helps avoid confusion!). The wine comes in slightly or fully fizzy styles—frizzante or spumante, respectively—and is known for its white peach flavors and crisp acidity. The best come from Prosecco di Conegliano-Valdobbiadene (co-ne-liano val-do-bi-ah-deneh). For a still white wine, grab a bottle of Soave (the region) made with garganega (gahr-gah-neh-gah) and trebbiano grapes. Fresh and crisp, this is another great sipping wine.

Take a deep breath as we move onto the region's red wines: the explanation gets a little circular! The most entry-level of these reds is Valpolicella, Italy's answer to Beaujolais—and not just for the banana flavors that infuse both wines. This fruity wine goes down easy, with additional flavors of blueberry and sour cherry. It stands alone or is a good match with food. Its

Amarone grapes left to shrivel on racks before fermentation and bottling.

opposite is Amarone della Valpolicella— colloquially called Amarone— that is made with grapes that have been dried and shriveled over several months, concentrating both the sugars and flavors. But this is by no means a sweet wine: intense and compelling are much better descriptors. That "raisiny" is a characteristic flavor should come as no surprise, but also look for notes of black fruit, earth, or leather. These are most certainly wines to pair with food.

Now we come to ripasso della valpolicella, a wine that lies squarely between valpolicella and amarone in terms of style. This wine is made more complex and tannic by the addition of the grape skins and other goop left over from a batch of amarone that's done fermenting. It's much tastier than it sounds, and, to be fair, winemaking isn't always pretty! Finally, if you like dessert wine, a fourth style called recioto (re-chee-oto) della valpolicella is a sweet version of Amarone.

Dizzy yet?

Attack of the Clones?

Rest assured that a grape clone isn't some sort of viticultural Frankenstein created in a lab. First off, natural mutations happen in grapes all the time, most of them unnoticeable. But some of these— say, a resistance to fungus or a particular flavor—are desirable. A clone happens when a vintner takes a cutting from a desired plant and uses it to propagate more vines with its qualities.

Other Wine Regions in Italy

There are twenty wine regions in Italy, but many of the wines made therein are either undistinguished, meant for local consumption, or not produced in large enough numbers for export—but several of these wines are worth checking out. If sparkling wine is your drink of choice, look for a franciacorta, from the northern Lombardy region. This is Italy's most prestigious bubbly, with a depth and finesse lacking in prosecco or moscato, which are designed to be more lighthearted. Instead, franciacorta is crafted more along the style of Champagne, its creamy roundness amplified with notes of bread, lemon, hay, and nuts. The native varietal vermentino makes refreshing white wines for summer. The best of them have notes of peach, lemon, citrus, and a touch of the sea. Look for vermentino di Sardegna (from the island of Sardinia) or colli di luni (from the northern Liguria region) on the label.

The red wines worth mentioning are quite diverse. From Sicily, nero d'avola (both the grape and wine name) is cozy and warming, yet big and juicy, with notes of pepper and blackberry. The final wines worth mentioning showcase how one grape—in this case, aglianico—can make two very different-tasting wines. Taurasi, from the Campania region, is full-bodied and modern with a combination of fruit and earth flavors. The aglianico del vulture, from neighboring Basilicata, is more rustic, with rich notes of chocolate and cherry. Both of these wines shine with food.

New Zealand

This country's wine history is fairly young. Sure, the first vines were established in the 1830s, but it wasn't until the 1970s that winemakers started to focus on quality and the wines began to have global impact. (Thank you, jet travel!)

And what an impact they have had! New Zealand vintners took the sauvignon blanc grape, worked some special alchemy, and came up with a wine that is neither too elegantly restrained nor too rounded and blowsy. In fact, these wines are considered by some to be the best sauvignon in the world.

How about them apples? (Grapes?)

The flip side of that coin is pinot noir, the red grape playing a (nearly) equal role as the country's top varietal. But, in the country's short winegrowing history, a number of other grapes have been planted and are slowly but surely grabbing attention for themselves.

The country is divided into two islands, with winegrowing spanning all the way from Northland at the tip of the North Island to Central Otago at the bottom of the South Island, the world's southernmost winegrowing region. In general, wines from the warmer North Island are riper, richer, and rounder, while wines from the cool southern appellations have more elegance and minerality, with strong structure and a certain leanness.

What You Need to Know

New Zealand wines are known for their vibrant intensity, food-friendliness, and general drinkability!

Grapes

In addition to sauvignon blanc, chardonnay and pinot gris are the most widely grown white grapes. Pinot noir is the most widely planted red grape, with cabernet and merlot trailing.

What to Look For

Let's start with the top dog, sauvignon blanc. These wines are known for their intensity, with aromas and flavors leaping out of the glass. You'll encounter notes like cut grass, fresh herbs, grapefruit, and tropical fruits like pineapple and mango. Wairarapa (why-ra-rappa) is the best spot for the most powerful versions of these wines, though sauvignon is most widely grown in Marlborough, and those wines are much easier to find. Either way, it's hard to go wrong.

Chardonnay from Auckland, Waikato, Gisbourne, and Hawke's Bay are quite bold and show tropical fruit notes, with a bright acidity cutting through the wine's opulent feel. For a (slightly) more restrained, peach-infused wine, try one from Marlborough.

Curiously enough, some of the best pinot gris come from the same regions as chardonnay. These wines, however, are aromatic and spicy with notes of crisp white fruit and honeysuckle, the latter giving the wine its luscious feel.

As for the reds, the two best regions for pinot are Marlborough and Central Otago. No surprise there—both are located on the cooler South Island. From Marlborough, the wines are full of dark cherry, plum, and spice notes—fairly classic flavors crafted in a fruitier style. Go farther south, though, and the wines develop a silky intensity that gives them old-world elegance.

Finally, would you have pegged New Zealand as a go-to spot for Bordeaux-style blends? Me neither, but it is! Primarily made with cabernet and merlot (sometimes with other varietals thrown in), these wines are bold and intense with a plumy elegance and lots of style. Seek out ones from Auckland or Hawke's Bay on the North Island and enjoy your new discovery!

NEW ZEALAND

Northland
Auckland
AUCKLAND
NORTH ISLAND
Waikato
Gisbourne
TASMAN SEA
Hawke's Bay
Wairarapa
Marlborough
WELLINGTON
SOUTH ISLAND
SOUTH PACIFIC OCEAN
CHRIST CHURCH
Central Otago

OREGON

PACIFIC OCEAN

WASHINGTON

COLUMBIA RIVER

Chehalem Mountains

Yamhill-Carlton

PORTLAND

McMinnville

Ribbon Ridge
Dundee Hills

SALEM

Eola-Amity
Hills

Willamette Valley

EUGENE

IDAHO

Umpqua Valley

Rogue River Valley

MEDFORD

CALIFORNIA

Oregon

Oregon's high profile as a pinot noir producer has always been inversely proportional to its production. This is unquestionably a region of small, handcrafted wines made by people with a sense of collaboration and community. It wasn't until the 1970s that wineries began to meaningfully reduce production of labrusca grapes—the species of native varietals known for their "foxy" musk—in favor of the European vinifera vines most common today. The state's winemaking pioneers ignored conventional wisdom (the experts believed that Oregon was too cold for grapegrowing –ha!), and a handful of intrepid vintners established their estates in the late 1960s. Their prescience was rewarded in 1979, when David Lett—one of the aforementioned pioneers—submitted a pinot noir from his Eyrie Vineyards in the Gault-Millau French Wine Olympiades. (Say that three times fast!) The wine placed in the top ten and was rated best overall pinot against some very tough French competition. People started to take notice. From its small start, the Oregon winemaking industry has grown to include sixteen AVAs and more than 300 wineries crafting wine from seventy-two different varietals. Wheee!

Willamette (will-am-itte) Valley

What You Need to Know

At roughly the same latitude (and similar climate) as Burgundy, the Willamette Valley is the place to go for some crazy delicious pinot noir.

Grapes

Pinot noir rules the roost, but white grapes pinot gris and chardonnay more than hold their own.

What to Look For

With a cool climate, it's no wonder that Willamette Valley winemakers produce pinot noir that rivals those from the great French region. These versions tend to marry the best of Old World and New World styles, creating wines that are fruity yet have an earthy depth that makes them a delight to drink. The Willamette Valley is the state's biggest appellation, but don't let its size fool you. Often, these wines are made with fruit sourced from one or more of six sub-AVAs, making wines that are greater than the sum of their parts. If you're looking for a pinot on the lighter side, the Willamette Valley is a good place to start. These wines show typical Oregon pinot flavors, including a combination of cherry, strawberry, and raspberry along with notes of mushroom, violet, and soft spices. For more complexity, look at the smaller AVAs within the valley. For example, pinot from the Dundee Hills has a distinct minerality and notes of violet, while wine from the Chehalem (she-ha-lem) Mountains is known for its spicy-cherry character and silky feel on the palate. These wines are all delightful on their own or paired with food. If you prefer more intensity in your glass, look for wines from Eola-Amity Hills or Yamhill-Carlton. Both are lush and aromatic, with an acidity that makes these perfect matches with food. Finally, the most intense, ageable Oregon pinots come from McMinnville and Ribbon Ridge. In addition to having higher tannins, these wines offer layered flavors and a crisp feel. A word to the wise: due to the area's small size and distinctive terroir, Ribbon Ridge wines are emerging as cult favorites!

More Details

Shockingly, there are more to reds in Oregon than pinot! While that sumptuous grape dominates the Willamette Valley, it's possible to find other delightful reds from other parts of the state. In particular, look for merlot and cabernet from the Rogue River Valley. These wines lean toward Bordeaux in style, mixing warm fruit notes with a crisp texture. For something completely different (albeit harder to find), seek out fruity, peppery syrah from the Umpqua Valley. At this point, you might be asking if there are any white wines in Oregon. The answer is, of course there are! Though they fly under the radar screen (a bit of an understatement), Oregon's white wines are pretty awesome—and a good value for the savvy shopper. In particular, look for chardonnay, pinot blanc, and riesling. Versions from the Willamette Valley and its smaller AVAs tend to be crisp and minerally with nice fruit flavors. Wines from warmer areas like the Rogue River Valley are generally rounder and no less fruity.

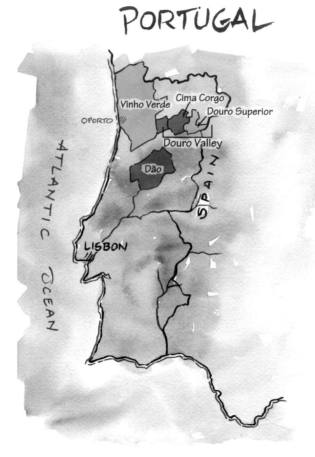

PORTUGAL

Vinho Verde

Cima Corgo

Douro Superior

OPORTO

Douro Valley

Dão

ATLANTIC OCEAN

SPAIN

LISBON

Portugal

When it comes to wine, Portugal is probably best known for Port, its flagship desert wine (rightly so), as well as (less rightly) Mateus and Lancers, the slightly sweet, slightly fizzy rosé wines that came in funny-shaped bottles and were global juggernauts in the 1970s. However, the mania for these wines inspired a handful of Port producers to experiment with dry wine production. This decision was, conveniently, also a way to enhance revenues by making use of grapes not suited for their flagship wine. As these pioneers saw success, the idea of producing quality dry wines eventually took hold throughout the country. Among the benefits of strong dry wine sales were upgraded vineyards and winemaking facilities, a boom in smaller vineyards, and, ultimately, more improved wines. Winemakers also have the advantage of making blends from 500-plus native varietals, ensuring that their wines taste like nothing else out there.

Vinho Verde

What You Need to Know

This slightly effervescent, green-tinged (but white) wine is the perfect accompaniment for summer.

Grapes

Alvarinho and loureiro (lurr-err-oh) are the most commonly used grapes in Vinho Verde.

What to Look For

These wines are neither expensive nor fine, and that's exactly as it should be. With their combination of low alcohol, crisp minerality, and fresh lemon-lime flavors, they go down ridiculously easily. In fact, on a warm summer day, it's entirely possible to drink a whole bottle without even realizing it.

Winemakers in Vinho Verde once trained vines on pergolas as a way to maximize space. Today, they just look lovely. Photo courtesy of Comissão de Viticultura da Região dos Vinhos Verdes.

(Not that that has ever happened to me.) Look for one that costs between seven to twelve dollars, and you'll be fully satisfied.

Douro

What You Need to Know

This area is considered Portugal's premium wine region, both for both its Port and dry red wines.

Grapes

The main red grapes grown here are touriga nacional, tinta barroca, tinta cão, tinta roriz, and touriga franca.

What to Look For

The red wines are opulent and complex, with purple flavors (think violet, blackberry, and plum), complemented by sweet spices and earthy undertones. The best labels are from Douro Superior and Cima Corgo, where most of the well-known quintas (wine estates) are located. Given that table wine wasn't produced there until 1952, it's ironic that grapes considered inferior to Port—such as those from a too-cold vintage —are actually excellent grapes for making dry wines.

Dão

What You Need to Know

Wines from this region are food-friendly and offer that oh-so-desirable combination of quality and value.

Grapes

Touriga nacional, tinta roriz, jaen (hine), and alfrocheiro preto (alfra-shero prato) are the primary red grapes used.

What to Look For

Dão wines are very similar to Burgundy's pinot noirs in several respects, though one is not likely to confuse them in a blind tasting. They are quite balanced and elegant, with flavors that are less fruity (though black fruit flavors are certainly evident) and more savory-earthy (think cocoa, tea, and mushrooms). With their high acidity, these wines pair well with a wide range of foods. They lean toward the tannic side so generally age well. The top reserve wines may have the Dão Nobre ("Noble Dão") designation, though for an everyday wine, pretty much any bottle from this region is a good choice.

Port

What You Need to Know

Port is generally a sweet red wine, typically served on its own as dessert or as an accompaniment to one.

Grapes

By law, winemakers are allowed to use any of hundreds of varietals to make Port, but by and large they stick with a top five: touriga nacional, tinta barroca, tinta cão, tinta roriz, and touriga franca.

What to Look For

The styles of Port vary widely, from sweet to semidry to dry. And, while most are red, white and rosé versions can also be found. To help you decide, to follow is a basic rundown of the major red styles. (Though tasting for yourself is always the best way to choose one—wink, wink!)

Ruby: This is the least expensive and most widely produced style. It is generally crafted in cement vats or stainless-steel tanks to maintain its young, fruity character.

Tawny: This Port is basically a ruby that's spent time in a barrel, giving it greater dimension and heft. The most basic wines spend only a couple of years in the barrel and are released simply as "tawny." However, you might see "10/20/30/40 Year" indicated on a label. These wines are blends of Port from several different vintages. The number doesn't indicate the wine's actual age, but the age the wine is supposed to taste like. Tawny Port flavors will range from fruity, nutty, or figgy to earthy, chocolaty, and leathery. Those in the know suggest that the twenty-year tawnies offer the best combination of flavor and value.

Colheita (a.k.a. Single Harvest Reserve): This is a tawny Port made with fruit from a single year. While the label will indicate the vintage, it is different from a vintage Port. Colheita (col-yay-tah) may spend anywhere from seven to twenty or more years barrel-aging before being bottled for release, while vintage Port is typically bottled after about eighteen months in the barrel. You still get a lot of the sweet, nutty, dried fruit qualities of a blended tawny, but with the additional depth and finesse of a vintage Port. As a result, colheita often is more affordable than a true vintage wine.

Late Bottle Vintage (LBV): Originally, this style of Port was made by mistake. The wine was designated for vintage status but was kept in the barrel longer than planned. The oops turned into an opportunity, and LBV was created. The wine is from a single year and is crafted to be lighter-bodied and more accessible than a vintage Port. It is fruity and bright, ready to drink right away.

Vintage: Only 2 percent of Port production achieves this status. A vintage Port is declared only in exceptional years, and it is up to the individual Port house to determine if the harvest is vintage-worthy. Vintage Port is left in barrel no longer than two and a half years but needs from ten to forty years in a bottle before it is ready to drink. This wine is definitely a heavy hitter, with notes of black fruit, chocolate, nuts, coffee, and spice.

Rabelo boats: The old-school way of transporting Port to market.

Spain

Winemaking has been taking place in Spain since 4000 to 3000 BC. (Let that sink in for a moment!) The industry thrived through the Roman Empire, Moorish rule (though Islamic, the Moors apparently had mixed feelings about wine, as it was clearly cultivated, imbibed, and taxed), competition with New World wines (seriously!), and even the phylloxera epidemic that devastated French vineyards in the 19th century. It struggled mightily, however, in the 20th century, while Spain endured a civil war and the dictatorship of Franco. During these years, what industry there was largely focused on quantity over quality. Thankfully, the mid 1970s saw the death of said dictator and the reemergence of capitalism. The new flow of money helped create an urban class interested in fine dining and wine. Add to that Spain's entry into the European Union, and the country's winemakers began replanting, modernizing, and improving the quality and image of Spanish wines. As a result, Spanish wines are now known for offering a one-two punch of great taste and good value.

Spain has two ways of classifying wines. Like much of Europe, the first divides them into quality levels, starting with the lowest, which designates table wine. The top two levels indicate quality and are overseen by a regulating body. Most of these wines have Denominación de Origen (DO) status. Only two regions have achieved the highest level, Denominación de Origen Calificada (DOCa), which indicates areas of special distinction. The second classification gives age designations to the wines. The term "joven" (ho-ven) indicates wine sold the year after it was harvested, having spent little to no time in a barrel. Designed for early drinking, these wines are typically light and fruity. Crianza wines must be aged for at least two and a half years and spend six months in oak (one year for DOCa wines) before they are released. Reserva wines are

SPAIN

aged for a minimum of three and a half years, at least one and a half years of that time in oak. Gran Reserva wines are made in great vintages or from selected grapes in very good vintages. They must be aged for five years (two in oak) before being released. This designation indicates a wine with more depth and complexity, with flavors tending toward earthy rather than fruity. Many winemakers are allowed to exceed these minimum aging requirements, some doing so by many years. While Spain is rightly known for its red wines, the country also makes some delicious, drinkable white wines that offer terrific alternatives to the typical chardonnay or sauvignon blanc.

Navarra

What You Need to Know

This region makes very modern-style red and rosé wines.

Grapes

Garnacha (grenache) and tempranillo are the primary grapes grown, though good cabernet sauvignon and merlot can be found here, too.

What to Look For

Navarra's winemakers combine a penchant for quality with an experimental flair, so these wines come in a variety of styles. As a whole, they are typically fresh and fruity, tending toward full-bodied. Look for a crianza for a young wine, or a single-varietal garnacha for a more upscale option. Whichever style you prefer, these are all terrifically food-friendly wines.

Penedès

What You Need to Know

This area is cava territory, home to a sparkling wine that's a great alternative to Champagne.

Grapes

The three primary grapes grown here are macabeo, xarello, and parellada. (The latter are pronounced shar-ell-oh and pair-ee-yahda, respectively).

What to Look For

Cava is a great choice for easygoing, value-oriented bubbly. Typically made with a combination of three native grapes, some of these wines include other Spanish varietals and/or the classic Champagne grapes of chardonnay and pinot noir in the bottle. This wine is hallmarked by its distinctly earthy tone and slightly spicy flavor. It is surprisingly versatile, matching well with a wide range of foods, particularly seafood and spicy cuisine. It also is nice to drink at the end of a meal, with lighter-style desserts. It's hard to go wrong picking one: a good cava can be had for fifteen dollars or less. That said, bottles labeled Gran Reserva have additional aging and offer more complexity and depth—and are commensurately more expensive. In this case, the reserva designation has no meaning except to the winemaker.

Priorat

What You Need to Know

These red wines are powerful, age-worthy, and among Spain's most expensive. These are serious wines for serious wine drinkers.

Grapes

Garnacha tinta is the most important grape used in this wine, though cariñea plays an important supporting role.

What to Look For

Priorat is a difficult region for cultivating grapes. The slate-influenced licorella soil forces vines to dig deep for water, so yields are low. In addition, vineyards are planted on steep mountain slopes, requiring intense work by hand to grow and harvest the fruit. However, the rewards for these efforts are tremendous. These wines are particularly rich, flavorful, and intense with notes of purple fruits, particularly blackberry and plum. Most have the snuff to age for many years, with the flavors turning over time to earth and leather. For the collector, it's worth the investment to tuck away some bottles for a few years. However, if you're more the instant gratification type, look for a joven or crianza, or an older vintage that's ready to drink. Finally, for something a little different, check out cabernet or syrah from the region. Both varietals have an affinity for the region's harsh soils and climate, offering big, bold wines with lots of savory olive, earth, dark fruit, and spice notes.

Rías Baixas (ree-ahs buy-shuss)

What You Need to Know

This region's fragrant, fruity albariño wines make a lovely alternative to chardonnay.

Grapes

Albariño is the primary grape grown here, though other native varietals are allowed in the wines.

What to Look For

Winemakers in Rías Baixas, like in much of Spain, lean toward the experimental. For example, many cultivate their own yeast to start fermentation so the particular characteristics of these wines will vary. However, you can expect a very fragrant, stylish wine with notes of lemon, white peach, melon, mango, and honeysuckle. With their crisp minerality and medium body, these wines are delicious solo or with food, though they have a particular affinity for spicy cuisine. In order to have the Rías Baixas designation, the wine must be at least 70 percent albariño. For something a little more special, look for "adegas" on the label. It's the equivalent of bodegas or cellar and often indicates an artisanal producer.

Ribera del Duero

What You Need to Know

The red wines from this area are well made and complex.

Grapes

Tempranillo is the primary grape grown here, though five other authorized varietals can also be used.

What to Look For

Wines from Ribera Del Duero have gotten quite a reputation in recent years—in the best possible way! Home to cult winery Vega Sicilia, one of Spain's oldest producers, the area has seen the number of bodegas explode in the past thirty years. These aromatic wines are crafted in a modern style, offering a combination of power and elegance. Layered and complex, these wines are hallmarked by dark spice flavors accented with notes of mulberry and blackberry. Reserva and Gran Reserva wines can age remarkably for several years, whereas the youngest ones should be consumed right away. Ribera Del Duero wines are best served with food.

Rioja (ree-oh-ha)

What You Need to Know

This area is renowned for its elegant, intense red wines. This area's white wines are lesser known, but no less interesting.

Grapes

Tempranillo and garnacha are the primary red grapes found here, whereas the main white grapes include viura, malvasia, and garnacha blanca.

What to Look For

Rioja's red wines are typically balanced with a nice depth and finesse. They are fruity and young, gaining a velvety texture with age, and are generally medium-to full-bodied. Common flavors include cherry, tobacco, herbs, plum, and vanilla. The appellation is divided into three subzones, but its oldest and best vineyards are concentrated in Rioja Alta. These grapes produce elegant yet full-bodied wines with noted concentrations and smooth textures. Wines from Rioja Alavesa are, crazily, even firmer and fuller-bodied than those from its neighboring zone, with a distinct fruitiness to them. Rioja Baja is the third subzone. These wines typically have a higher alcohol content and are most often used for blending. Many bodegas use fruit from all three regions, adjusting the blends each year to best showcase the fruit. Rioja's white wines tend to be both underrated and hard to find but are fresh and fruity with a distinct nutty-caramel quality that makes them worth seeking out.

Rueda

What You Need to Know

This well-regarded region is known for producing white wines that are delicious on their own or with food.

Grapes

Verdejo is the native varietal here, though other grapes are permitted in the blend.

What to Look For

Verdejo is known for its floral aromas, while the flavors lean toward the herbal. It's like a less exuberant sauvignon blanc, with a fuller, richer feel on the palate. This wine is delicious on its own but quite versatile with food. Your best bet for a pick from this region is a rueda superior, which must contain at least 75 percent verdejo.

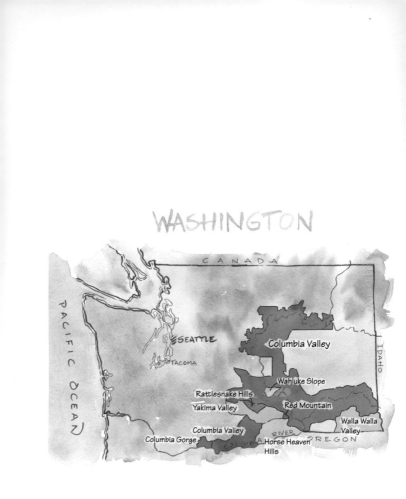

WASHINGTON

CANADA

PACIFIC OCEAN

SEATTLE
TACOMA

Columbia Valley

Wahluke Slope

Rattlesnake Hills
Red Mountain

Yakima Valley

Walla Walla
Valley

Columbia Valley

RIVER

Columbia Gorge

COLUMBIA

OREGON

Horse Heaven
Hills

IDAHO

Washington State

Though grapes were first planted in Washington in 1825, the state's first winery wasn't established until 1860. In that fashion, the industry's overall growth happened pretty slowly: In 1978, only 2,500 acres of vines were planted. Perhaps that's why Washington isn't the first place people think of for wine. Little do they know they are missing out. Though the industry is still getting its footing, the area now boasts over 40,000 acres under vine. Production is split almost evenly between red and white wines, and it's pretty easy to find superb wines and good values from both types of grape.

What You Need to Know

White wines are delicious, but the red wines are even better—merlot and cabernet sauvignon in particular.

Grapes

Chardonnay and riesling are the most widely planted whites, while cabernet sauvignon is the most widely planted red, followed by merlot and syrah. More than thirty varietals are grown throughout the state.

What to Look For

Fans of chardonnay should look for labels from the Yakima Valley, Columbia Gorge, or Horse Heaven Hills. These wines show a range of flavors from green apple to peach to pineapple. But that's not the only white grape game in town. Two other grapes— riesling and gewürztraminer—are worth finding. The smaller appellations of Columbia Gorge,

Rattlesnake Hills, and Horse Heaven Hills are your best bets for these crisp, citrusy-peachy wines. Terrific cabernet and merlot can be found from many of the same appellations. The cabernet is very classic in style, with notes of black cherry and cassis, while the merlot shows less of its classic plum flavor as much as notes of red fruits, chocolate, and mint. Wines from the Yakima Valley, Horse Heaven Hills, Wahluke Slope, and Rattlesnake Hills will all be divine. Syrah is showcased particularly well in Washington's vineyards, where it creates a dark, tannic, minerally wine with savory notes of earth, olives, bacon, and smoke. The syrah-producing appellations include Wahluke Slope, Walla Walla Valley, and Red Mountain. The Columbia Valley is the state's overarching appellation, containing ten official subregions within its borders. While it may not always be the best source for this state's wine, it is nonetheless a good one, particularly if you are on a budget or choosing from a limited selection of wines.

The Finale
Put a Cork in It

My students want to tell me this a lot, given that they have to listen to me talk for a good twenty to thirty minutes before they can start tasting wine. Luckily, you've had the option to sip as you read, and I hope you've learned a lot along the way. Maybe you now have a new favorite grape, or a different perspective on your go-to vino. Perhaps you're even the person your friends automatically turn to when ordering wine at a restaurant, or you have a newfound confidence as you browse through a wine store. As you continue to explore the world of wine, I leave you with my thanks for reading this book and finish with a few parting words:

Take this book, and the knowledge you've gained, and use it for good, not evil.

Remember which wine rules to follow religiously, and those that you can bend so far they break.

Don't mock those loving on white zinfandel. Think of it as a gateway wine, and help them get over the threshold.

Always remain open to trying new wines. What's in the bottle just might surprise you.

Cheers!

Glossary

Acidity: The amount of acid in a wine. There are three primary acids: tartaric, malic, and citric. Acidity makes your mouth water, feels crisp and refreshing on the palate, and is one of the qualities that make a wine food-friendly.

Age (noun): Simply how old a wine is, based on the vintage date.

Age (verb): A wine's ability to improve over time in the bottle. Few wines truly age, though they will keep in the bottle for three to five years. The ones that are age-worthy include high-end wines from Bordeaux, Napa, and Barolo.

Appellation: A legally defined area where wine grapes are grown.

AVA: American Viticultural Area, or the legal appellations in the US.

Balance: When a wine's acidity, tannins, and fruit are in harmony.

Barrel: A method of aging wine before it is put into bottle. Barrels are made of French, American, or Slovenian oak. This treatment can add flavors, soften tannins, and create a silky texture. A typical barrel holds about sixty gallons of wine, or three hundred bottles.

Biodynamic: A holistic way of farming that encompasses not just growing grapes, but processing them, as well. The ideas are based on the work of Rudolf Steiner. It combines using natural ingredients in the vineyards (i.e., no chemicals or even things like commercial yeast) with spiritual elements, such as harvesting grapes on "fruit days" and pruning on "root days." While there is no scientific way to measure it, people say that biodynamic wines have more vibrant flavors and a greater sense of "place."

Bowl: The part of a wineglass that holds the wine.

Brix: The amount of sugar in a grape, which determines a wine's potential alcohol. (Remember that in winemaking, sugar + yeast = alcohol!)

Capsule: The foil or wax at the top of a wine bottle protecting the cork.

Cement Vat: An old-school way of fermenting and/or aging wine that is making a small comeback. It is beneficial because it combines the neutrality of stainless steel with the breathability of oak.

Clone: A variation on a grape that is created when a grower finds a vine with a particular quality she or he wants to replicate, such as resistance to disease or a thicker skin. The clone is created simply by taking and propagating a cutting or bud from the "mother" plant.

Cuvée: Another word for blend. A cuvée might contain wines from different grapes, vintages, or vineyards.

Decanter: A glass container designed to help aerate wine before it is served, bringing out its flavors and aromas.

Distributor: A company that allocates and delivers wine to retail stores. Distributors are typically the middle link between an importer and a retailer.

Fermentation: The process that uses yeast to convert grape juice to wine. Fermentation can last anywhere from five to fourteen days and usually takes place in stainless-steel tanks or wooden vats. Some wines spend another five to ten days in secondary fermentation, which takes place in a different vessel from primary fermentation. The classic example of this is in Champagne, where secondary fermentation happens in the bottle.

Galets: Small stones in the vineyards that are beneficial because they absorb heat during the day and reflect it back onto the vines at night, keeping them warm as outside temperatures cool. They are prevalent in the Rhône Valley, particularly Châteauneuf du Pape.

Grafting: A process of joining the tissues of two plants so they can grow together. Many vitis vinifera vines were grafted onto American rootstock to combat the phylloxera louse.

Harvest: The time of year when wine grapes are picked. Exact timing varies, but it usually happens sometime between August and October in the northern hemisphere and February and April in the southern hemisphere.

Hectare: A metric unit used to describe the size of a vineyard. One hectare is 10,000 square meters and equal to 2.47 acres.

Importer: A company that brings wine into the US.

Malolactic Fermentation: A process in winemaking that converts harsh malic acid (think apples) into softer lactic acid (think milk). This is often done as a secondary fermentation. Most red wines undergo this process as do certain white wines, particularly chardonnay. Wines that have gone through this process tend to be round and creamy and can show flavors of hazelnut and dried fruit (in white wines) or chocolate, spice, or smoke (in red wines). Sometimes referred to as MLF or malo.

Meniscus: The clear, watery part at the edge of a wine. You can see it best by putting some wine in a glass, holding it at an angle between you and a piece of white paper, and looking down at the far side of the wine glass.

Microclimate: The distinctive climate of a smaller area within an appellation.

Nonvintage: Generally refers to Champagne but can apply to any wine whose grapes come from two or more vintages. No year will appear on the label.

Oak: The favored wood for fermenting and aging wine. Oak treatment helps shape a wine's color, flavors, texture, and tannins.

Old Vine: This typically refers to zinfandel grapevines that are fifty or more years old. Vines that are eighty or older are sometimes called ancient vines They are coveted because their fruit makes wines that are particularly deep, concentrated, and flavorful.

Organic: A designation that a wine's grapes were grown without use of chemical or artificial fertilizers, pesticides, fungicides, or herbicides. There are typically very strict rules that wineries must follow to be certified organic.

Oxidation: Generally considered a wine fault, occurring when a wine has too much exposure to oxygen and loses color, flavor, and/or aroma.

Palate: The ability to discern a wine's flavor and texture.

Phylloxera: A small insect that feeds on the roots and leaves of grapevines, eventually killing the plant. Phylloxera destroyed most of Europe's grapevines in the late 19th century. American vine species (vitis labrusca) are resistant to the louse, and, as a result, most European grapevines are grafted onto American rootstock. This and a process called hybridization—the breeding of vitis vinifera with resistant species—are the only known ways to combat the louse.

Residual Sugar: What is left of the grape's natural sugar at the end of fermentation. A dry wine typically has two to three grams per liter (g/l) of sugar, while sweet wines start at thirty g/l but can have as much as 200 g/l or more! Often abbreviated as RS.

Rootstock: The root system of the plant.

Soil: Dirt, obviously. In winegrowing, the minerals and other natural elements contained in different soils impart different characteristics to the wine. For example, wines from sandy soils tend to be lighter in color, acidity, and tannin, while many bold, savory wines come from areas with clay soils. Different grapes, too, thrive in different soils.

Sommelier: The person in a restaurant who specializes in wine service.

Sparkling Wine: Wine that has gone through a secondary fermentation to produce bubbles but was not produced in France's Champagne region.

Stainless-Steel Vats: Large metal containers used to ferment and/or age wine. The benefit of stainless is its neutrality, allowing a wine's flavors to come forward without the influence of oak.

Sulfite: A preservative also known as SO2, or sulfur dioxide. Sulfites occur naturally as part of the fermentation process but can also be added to a wine after fermentation. A bottle must be labeled "contains sulfites" if it has more than ten parts per million of SO2. Many people think organic wines contain no sulfites, but that's not true. Organic wines simply have no *added* sulfites.

Sustainable: A method of farming that seeks to preserve and protect natural and human resources.

Tannin: Tannins are a naturally occurring polyphenol found in fruit skins. It might be best to think of them as a texture: that fuzzy, cottony feel your teeth sometimes get when drinking wine. Tannins allow wines to age, one reason highly tannic wines like cabernet and nebbiolo keep so well for so long.

Terroir: The French notion that a grapevine's physical environment—such as soil, weather, and elevation— impacts a wine's flavors and aromas.

Toast: The char level inside a wine barrel. The degree of toast imparts a range of aromas and flavors on the wine.

Varietal: A single, specified type of grape, such as syrah or riesling.

Vintage: The year the grapes were harvested. It typically appears on the label, indicating that most to all of the fruit in the wine comes from that year.

Viticulture: The science, production, and study of grapes.

Vitis Labrusca: A species of grapevines native to the eastern parts of North America. Wines made from these grapes are known for their distinctive musky character.

Vitis Vinifera: The species of European wine grapes (they originated in the Mediterranean, central Europe, and southwestern Asia) we know and love, including cabernet, chardonnay, merlot, sauvignon blanc, riesling, and pinot noir.

Yield: No, not a traffic sign! Yield is the ratio of grapes per vine or vines per acre (or hectare) in a vineyard. A low yield means fewer grapes or vines and high yield means more grapes. Lower yield is generally considered better, because a vine can concentrate more of its energy on less fruit, making the grapes more flavorful and concentrated. The same idea applies to the number of vines in a vineyard. Typical yields for quality wines are about five tons per acre or less (it's about three in Bordeaux). A high-yield vineyard will produce about ten tons of grapes per acre. How much does one ton get you? Roughly seven hundred bottles of wine, so that offers some perspective on winemaking math!

About the Author

With over fifteen years of experience in the food and wine industry, Kathleen Bershad has honed the art of matching people with wine. The enthusiasm she has for helping clients discover and learn about wine led her to establish her consulting practice, Fine Wine Concierge. Kathleen helps clients with all their wine needs, including buying wine to enjoy or collect, selling part or all of cellars, organizing wine cellars and creating inventories thereof, and hosting fun and educational tasting classes. She developed her expertise by working as a food writer and restaurant reviewer, a retail store manager, a sales associate for a boutique wine importer/distributor, and a buyer and writer for a top retail store and wine club in New York City. Kathleen earned her Sommelier Certification from the American Sommelier Association. She also has an undergraduate degree in communications from Trinity University.

Acknowledgments

Writing this book was a long and solitary process. But it wouldn't be here without the support and expertise of some very fabulous people.

First off, to Deborah Schneider, who was not only one of those students who pushed me as a teacher, but was, as my literary agent, an early champion of this book.

Her colleague Penelope Burns also deserves a thank-you, not only for her support and efforts on my behalf, but also for asking the innocent question, "Have you considered writing a conclusion?" (No, and one was definitely needed!)

Another big thanks to Radha McLean for her sharp editing eye and spot-on suggestions for making my writing (and therefore this book!) even better.

Daria Laucello helped me get over the finish line, offering her design advice, inspiration, and confidence in this book.

Credit must also be given to Jeffery Mathison for creating the beautiful maps that appear throughout these pages. They were done through a combination of hand drawing and computer magic. Thank you for them!

A million thank-yous are due to Nicole Mele at Skyhorse Publishing for finding my book proposal in their submissions basket! I am so glad you wanted to publish it, and it has been a delight to work with you through this process.

Also hugs, kisses, and a big glass of pinot noir to Susan Nolan for reading early versions of the book and helping give it its voice. It wouldn't have made it this far without you.

To my pop, Max McCullough, and stepmom, Francie Fite, for always being in my corner (and their infinite supply of parental pride!).

Next, I need to give a shout-out to my brother-in-law, William Bershad, who shamelessly asked if he would be in the acknowledgments section.

And last, but definitely not least, to my husband, Jeff, for his never-ending support and encouragement; and to our kids, Sarah and Josh, who never take anything too seriously.

Notes